Water Demand Management
in the
City of the Future

Water Demand Management *in the* City of the Future

– Selected Tools and Instruments for Practitioners –

Water, Engineering and Development Centre
Loughborough University
2011

Water, Engineering and Development Centre,
Loughborough University,
Leicestershire, LE11 3TU, UK

© WEDC, Loughborough University, 2011

ISBN 13 Paperback: 978 1 84380 136 8
ISBN Ebook: 9781788533676
Book DOI: http://dx.doi.org/10.3362/9781788533676

A catalogue record for this book is available from the British Library.

Kayaga, S. and Smout, I. (2011)
Water Demand Management in the City of the Future

WEDC (The Water, Engineering and Development Centre) at Loughborough University
in the UK is one of the world's leading institutions concerned with education, training,
research and consultancy for the planning, provision and management of physical
infrastructure for development in low- and middleincome countries.

This edition is reprinted and distributed by Practical Action Publishing.
Since 1974, Practical Action Publishing has published and disseminated books and
information in support of international development work throughout the world.
Practical Action Publishing trades only in support of its parent charity objectives and
any profits are covenanted back to Practical Action (Charity Reg. No. 247257, Group
VAT Registration No. 880 9924 76).

Designed, illustrated and produced by
Glenda McMahon, Rod Shaw and Ken Chatterton

Find out more about WEDC Publications online at:
http://www.lboro.ac.uk/wedc/publications/

Acknowledgements

This book was prepared within the framework of the European research project SWITCH (Sustainable Urban Water Management Improves Tomorrow's City's Health). SWITCH was supported by the European Commission under the 6th Framework Programme and contributes to the thematic priority area of "Global Change and Ecosystems" [1.1.6.3] Contract no 018530-2.

We are grateful to Prof. Stuart White, Andrea Turner and the team at the Institute for Sustainable Futures, University of Technology, Sydney for their guidance, support and provision of materials on Integrated Resource Planning and Water Demand Management. We are also grateful to other members of the SWITCH International Panel of Experts on Water Demand Management for their invaluable contributions. These were Prof. Kala Vairavamoorthy; Dr Cyrus Njiru; Roland Liemberger; Bambos Charalambous; Dr Bekithemba Gumbo; Maria do Céu Almeida; Prof. David Butler; Nicole Poole; Rob Westcott; Dr. Md. Abdul Jalil, Mary Ann Dickinson; Hannes Buckle, Tony Gregg and Malcolm Farley.

Our thanks go to key stakeholders that assisted in data collection and supported the fieldwork in Zaragoza, Spain; Accra, Ghana; Alexandria, Egypt; and Kampala, Uganda. The following people deserve special mention: Javier Celma, Joaquin Garcia Lucea, Prof. Pilar Egea, Prof. Ramon Barberan Orti, Alfonso Marques, Maria Rojo from Zaragoza; Dr Kwabena Nyarko, Prof. Esi Awuah, Bertha Darteh, Francis Lamptey, Henrietta Osei-Tutu, John Gyansah, Kweku Botwe and Kenneth Agbettoh, from Accra; Dr Khaled Abuzeid, Eng. Nadia Abdou, Eng. Hanan Taha, Lama El Hatow, Ahmed Essam and Omar El Badawy from Alexandria; and Eng. Harrison Mutikanga and Willy Nuwagaba from Kampala.

We are most grateful to Carol Howe and Dr Bekithemba Gumbo for their advice and constructive review of the document. Finally, we are grateful to Patricia Jackson for her meticulous editing work; and to Rod Shaw and Glenda McMahon for their efficient contribution to the design and publication process.

List of contributors

Editors/Chapter authors

Dr Sam Kayaga is a Chartered Water Engineer and currently Lecturer/ Programme Manager at the Water, Engineering and development Centre (WEDC) of Loughborough University (UK). His main research areas are sustainable urban water management in the context of integrated resource planning, and provision of water/sanitation services to the poor and those un-served. He was Work Package Leader and Principal Investigator for the SWITCH Project research work on Water Demand Management. Prior to joining WEDC in 2002, he worked as an urban water and sanitation engineer/manager in Uganda for 18 years.

Ian Smout is a Chartered Civil Engineer who has worked on water management in developing countries since 1974, comprising 13 years with an international consultancy firm and 23 years with the Water Engineering and Development Centre (WEDC), Loughborough University. He has carried out research and consultancy assignments around the world, including fieldwork on water management from an interdisciplinary perspective in 14 developing countries, covering water resources, irrigation, water supply and sanitation and institutional development. He also has considerable experience in programme/project planning and management and in capacity development. He was Director of WEDC, 2002-2008, and a member of the Management Team of the EU-funded SWITCH project, 2007-2011. In his personal capacity he became Chair of RedR UK in 2010, an international charity that provides professional people and skills for disaster relief.

Foreword author

Dr Bekithemba Gumbo is the Director of Cap-Net, a UNDP Programme on capacity building in sustainable water management. Formerly he was the Manager of WaterNet, a Southern and Eastern Africa network affiliated to Cap-Net. In his most recent assignment Dr Gumbo held the position of Project Manager for a Southern Africa Development Community regional water demand management programme being implemented by the Development Bank of Southern Africa. He was a Member of the International Panel of Experts for the EU-funded SWITCH Project.

Chapter authors

Prof. Kala Vairavamoorthy is currently a professor at the Faculty of Civil and Environmental Engineering and Director of the School of Global Sustainability at the University of South Florida, USA. His research interests are in development and application of risk-based decision support systems and optimization tools for the design, operation and management of water-related infrastructure systems. He has a PhD in Environmental and Water Resources Engineering and an MSc in Environmental Engineering from Imperial College London. Previously, he was Professor at the University of Birmingham (UK), and at UNESCO-IHE (Netherlands) respectively. He was Scientific Director of the five-year EU-funded integrated project on Sustainable Urban Water management Improves Tomorrow's Cities' Health (SWITCH).

Dr Assela Pathirana is a Senior Lecturer in Urban Drainage and Sewerage at UNESCO-IHE Delft. Assela has strong background in numerical modelling, parallel computing, database systems, GIS and information and communication technology tools. His current research interests are focused on the interactions between the urban environment, atmosphere and hydrological cycle, which include: climate change, scaling with special emphasis on translating climatic forces to drivers of changes in urban-scale hydrology, single and multi-objective optimization in urban water applications. He obtained his Master's and Doctoral degrees in Civil Engineering, specializing in hydrology and water resources engineering, from Tokyo University. Previously, Assela was a post doctoral fellow at Chuo University and worked as a senior research fellow at the United Nations University.

Jotham Ivan Sempewo is a doctoral student in the Civil Engineering Department of the University of Birmingham (UK), researching on the transitioning of urban water distribution systems. Jotham has an MSc in Municipal Water and Infrastructure and has a strong background in development of models and tools for sustainable design and operation of urban water infrastructure systems. Previously, Jotham worked as District Water Engineer in Uganda, involved in the design and management of urban water and sanitation infrastructure systems for various local governments and rural growth centres.

Seneshaw Tsegaye is a graduate research assistant and a doctoral student at the School of Global Sustainability at the University of South Florida, USA. His current research areas are integrated urban water management as well as resilient and adaptive infrastructures. The area of his PhD research is Flexible Urban Water Distribution Systems. He received an MSc in Integrated Urban Engineering from UNESCO-IHE, Institute for Water Education, the Netherlands and BSc in Civil Engineering from Addis Ababa University, Ethiopia. Prior to joining the University of South Florida, he worked as a graduate assistant in University of Birmingham, United Kingdom.

Daniel van Rooijen is currently a Water, Sanitation and Hygiene Officer at UNICEF regional offices in Nairobi, Kenya. He is also a doctoral candidate at Loughborough University (UK) and has recently worked as a Research Associate at Water, Engineering and Development Centre (WEDC), UK and International Water Management Institute (IWMI), Accra (Ghana). His PhD research focusses on the impact of urban water use on agriculture and the environment up- and downstream of large cities in developing countries.

Laurent Sainctavit is a researcher at the Fundación Ecología y Desarrollo, an international non-governmental organisation based in Zaragoza, Spain that works with various stakeholders to promote sustainable development that optimises economic, social and environmental benefits. He is a water treatment specialist with more than 15 years' experience in France and Spain. He has worked with Fundación Ecología y Desarrollo since 2000, and carries out research on how to improve urban water management processes, specifically focusing on industries, commercial establishments and institutional facilities.

Victor Bueno is a wastewater management specialist working for the Agenda 21 local office in Ayuntamiento De Zaragoza, the City Council of Zaragoza, Spain. He was also the local contact person for the SWITCH Project in the City Council of Zaragoza.

Foreword

The "City of the future" is perceived as consisting of neighbourhoods. This urban renaissance will include the provision of water supply, sanitation, solid wastes and storm drainage services at the lowest economically efficient level, by neighbourhood or combination of neighbourhoods. The emphasis will be on resource conservation and recycling, synergism between services, commercialisation of services (whether through public or private ownership), and multiple use of facilities for maximum public benefit.

The rapid rate of urbanisation is resulting in many cities and towns facing major challenges of providing their increasing populations with adequate and sustainable water services. To compound the problem, extensive parts of the developing world in particular are currently water stressed, and the available water resources for these cities are dwindling rapidly. Not only are these cities and towns now unable to reconcile the water requirements and the water resources, but also current utilisation is often both inefficient and ineffective. As a result, the role of water conservation and water demand management (WDM) measures for reduction of water loss and water utilisation in all spheres of the water sector is urgent.

Africa has the world's most rapid urbanisation growth averaging 3.3% from 2005-2010. Today most of the urban growth is in medium and small sized urban settlements. About two-thirds of the anticipated 290 million new urban dwellers in Africa up to 2025 will be in towns of less than 500,000. Today 72 % of urban Africans live in slums (compared to 46% in Asia and 30% in Latin America and the Caribbean). Progress toward the water and sanitation MDGs are not keeping up with the pace of urbanisation in most urban areas.

This publication "Water Demand Management in the City of the Future: Selected Tools and Instruments for Practitioners" is timely and presents a wealth of knowledge and experiences necessary in overcoming the constraints to adoption of water demand management measures and ultimately the realisation of sustainable cities of the future.

Municipalities, local authorities and water utilities still give priority to developing new water supply schemes if the opportunity arises and financing becomes available. Demand-oriented interventions as proposed in this guide present an alternative solution, as WDM require small engineering inputs, and relatively small financing deals.

In developing countries in particular water service providers are characterised by the following; poor budget allocations or meagre financial resources for any meaningful WDM or water loss management projects; non-revenue water averaging 45%; water tariffs below cost and hence under-recovery for operations and maintenance; absence of a niche or market space for private sector investments; lack of a credit history; complex institutional arrangements leading to perceived and real risks for WDM financing; and invisible WDM investments leading to lack of political support and commitment.

These factors have contributed towards poor and unreliable water services, bad customer satisfaction and negative public opinion. The urban poor end up carrying most of the burden, and a vicious cycle ensues.

The publication illustrates that the WDM process is highly demanding in terms of technical, financial, economic, political, social and managerial skills. Without these skills, tools and instruments even if WDM is implemented it is unlikely to be sustained as it needs constant operational attention and buy-in to ensure that water losses and wastage is reduced and stay reduced. The guidance book further illustrates with the help of case studies the need for a proper mix of the various ingredients (e.g. money, planning skills, technology, customer education and awareness) critical for WDM implementation.

Dr Bekithemba Gumbo,
Director of Cap-Net
a UNDP Programme on capacity
building in sustainable water management

Contents

Part 1

Introduction

1

Overview of the guidance book

Sam Kayaga

Why water demand management?

Cities, towns and other urban areas are increasingly facing challenges of providing water services for the growing urban population and expanding economic activities. While the population in many industrialized countries is either decreasing or constant, the population in most developing countries is increasing rapidly, resulting in an overall global population increase. The current global population is estimated to be 6.9 billion people, of which 82% live in developing countries (UN-HABITAT, 2009).

Yet the water resources have remained constant, and are receiving an increasing pollution load from the growing population. The rate of abstraction of freshwater has subsequently grown rapidly, resulting in steadily declining per capita water availability. For example, human water use increased by a factor of six in the past century and, it is estimated, that global water withdrawals will increase by about 35% between 1995 and 2020 (Andresen, Lorch & Rosegrant, 1997). While the world's freshwater supplies may be adequate to meet global demand for the near future, the freshwater is poorly distributed across countries, within countries and between seasons. Hence, practical distribution problems concerned with time, space and affordability lead to a widening gap between demand and supply in many parts of the world.

The water scarcity situation is compounded by the major impacts of climate change on the water resources, namely shorter duration of the precipitation seasons and an increase in hydrological extremes (Stern, 2007). Shorter precipitation seasons, coupled with overall larger annual precipitations lead to larger runoff volumes generated over shorter time intervals, which in turn creates complications in designing for storage and routing of floods.

Furthermore, the opportunity time for groundwater recharge is reduced, which undermines the efficiency of conjunctive utilization of surface water and groundwater. If these climate changes continue at current rates, there is predicted to be a serious reduction in dry-season water availability in many regions of the world within the next few decades. One recent study predicted that a temperature rise of 2°C might result in 1 - 4 billion people of developing countries experiencing water shortages (Stern, 2007).

The water scarcity situation will get worse in the world's urban areas, which have grown to the extent that, since early 2007, over half of the world's population have lived in urban areas (UN-HABITAT, 2006). Between 2010 and 2030, it is projected that urban population will increase from 2.57 billion to 3.95 billion, 94% of this increase expected to be in low-income countries (UN-HABITAT, 2009). Parallel with this growth in population, the demand for drinking water has been increasing rapidly in urban areas, in line with raising living standards. Yet the number of viable water resources in any region is limited and has to serve competing requirements such as domestic, industrial, irrigation, fishing, navigation, tourism, recreational, ecological demands and waste disposal/assimilation.

Faced by the situation described above, contemporary urban water managers, engineers, planners and policy makers are faced with enormous challenges of effectively managing the ever dwindling water resources to deliver water and sanitation services while minimizing the negative impacts on the environment. They need to change from the conventional urban water management approach in which the traditional response to the ever-increasing water demand is usually the development of new water sources. One way of responding to these global pressures on the water resources is application of Water Demand Management (WDM) concepts, which is the topic of this guidance book.

The research context

This guidance book is one of the outputs of a five-year research project entitled 'Sustainable Water management Improves Tomorrow's Cities' Health' (SWITCH). The EU-funded SWITCH project was conceived out of a realization that continued application of the conventional urban water management (UWM) concept will not deliver the required results in the future. The main objective of the SWITCH project was "the development, application and demonstration of a range of tested scientific, technological and socio-economic solutions and approaches that contribute to the achievement of the sustainable and effective UWM schemes in The City of the future (projected 30-50 years from now). The SWITCH project was a multi-disciplinary integrated research project that aimed at creating a paradigm shift in urban water management, so as to address the challenges faced by water managers, planners and policy makers in the city of the future.

The specific objectives of the SWITCH project were:

- to develop an overall strategic approach to achieve sustainable urban water management in the city of the future,
- to develop effective storm-water management options in the context of the hydrological cycle at urban and river basin level,
- to explore ways of providing effective water supply services for all at minimum impact for water resources and the environment at large,
- to develop effective sanitation and waste management options based on the principles of 'Cleaner Production',
- to integrate urban water services into the ecological and other productive functions of water at city and river basin level, and
- to develop innovative, effective and interactive institutional arrangements covering the entire urban water cycle in the urban and broader river basin setting.

The SWITCH Project used an integrated urban water management approach that allows urban water managers, planners and policy makers to plan and manage water supply, wastewater and storm water systems in a coordinated manner so as to minimise their impact on the natural environment, maximise their contribution to economic development, and contribute to the welfare of the community. The project approach consisted of assessing major change pressures that affect the state of urban water system at city, river basin and global levels; strategic planning based on a Learning Alliance process and directed at creative visioning, scenario identification and strategy development; carrying out action research to develop innovative technological options relevant for the city of the future; multiple-way learning between cities of industrialised and developing countries; and implementation of strategic urban management plans with full participation of government and non-government sectors.

The SWITCH project research and demonstration activities aimed to catalyse a paradigm shift in the management of the urban water cycle and build capacity for optimal integration of diversified supply, storm water and wastewater disposal, water demand management to encourage rational water use, reuse options and augmentation of self-purification of water resources, using natural systems. The subject of this guidance book is water demand management, one of the research work packages contributing to SWITCH's objectives of enhancing efficient water supply and water use for all. The overall objective of the SWITCH Project Work Package on water demand management was to develop and test holistic demand management tools, which will assist water service operators to effectively manage water demand in their water supply systems. To develop these tools, research was mainly carried out in Zaragoza (Spain), Alexandria (Egypt), Accra (Ghana) and Kampala (Uganda). Case studies were also drawn from other parts of the world.

What is the purpose of this guidance book?

This guidance book is to assist urban water managers, engineers, planners and other relevant urban water professionals to mainstream water demand management in the strategic planning process of the urban water service providers and cities. For the purpose of this book, water demand management is defined as the development and implementation of strategies, policies, measures or other initiatives aimed at influencing water demand, to achieve efficient and sustainable use of the scarce water resources (Savenije and van der Zaag, 2002). These actions may lead to improved efficiency in the water supply systems; efficient and rational water use in the customers' premises and/or potable water source substitution such as wastewater reuse and rainwater harvesting. This book focuses on activities geared towards higher efficiency of water supply systems and end water uses. Potable water substitution options were dealt with by the SWITCH Project under the research themes of storm water management and wastewater reuse, and the research findings have been documented under various deliverables (refer to http://www.switchurbanwater.eu/ for more details) such as Wenhua and Jianming (2008); Ellis and Revitt (2011); and Liang and van Dijk (2008).

This book builds on a resource titled 'Planning our future water resources: a guide to demand management in the context of Integrated Resource Planning', developed by the Institute for Sustainable Futures, University of Technology, Sydney (Turner et al, 2006). The book does not focus on how to carry out water demand management, as a few good resources already exist for this purpose. It is assumed that the target audience will be familiar with the concepts of water demand management, and the guidance book introduces selected tools and instruments for use in various water demand management programmes. The guidance book also provides several case studies where instruments for water demand management have been successfully applied, or research has been conducted to ascertain their potential for application. Since the tools developed are software-based, only summary descriptions of these tools are provided in this guidance book. The necessary files to run these tools are freely available at the SWITCH Project website.

The book is particularly concerned with the problems of water demand management in the cities of developing countries, which often have major supply limitations; poor infrastructure; high levels of physical and commercial losses; low institutional capacity; limited data on operations; but also face major inequities in supply between low-income and higher-income areas.

Structure of this guidance book

This guidance book is divided into three parts. The first part introduces the book and the principles of water demand management underpinning the material presented in the rest of the book. Chapter 1 provides the purpose and an overview of the book. Chapter 2 describes various definitions of water demand management, water demand management measures being undertaken in various parts of the world, and the benefits that have been obtained from these programmes. Chapter 3 describes principles of Integrated Resource Planning, a framework that was adopted by the SWITCH project to research water demand management.

Part 2 presents emerging water demand management tools developed under the SWITCH Project. Chapter 4 describes a generic demand management options model, which was developed using a VENSIM modelling shell that is freely available on the internet. Chapter 5 briefly describes the use of agent-based modelling to estimate household water demand, and explore optimal demand-side water management strategies. Chapter 6 presents a computer-based tool that was developed for optimal demarcation of complicated distribution piped networks into zones for monitoring water losses.

Part 3 describes examples of instruments that have been applied for water demand management, and presents case studies of implementing programmes for managing water demand. Chapter 7 provides a case study of developing a water-saving culture in Zaragoza, Spain through a partnership championed by a non-governmental organization, and composed of other stakeholders such as individual households, governmental institutions, and private sector organizations. Apart from general public education, a combination of economic instruments was applied in Zaragoza to contribute to the city's 'water-saving culture'. These instruments have been described in Chapter 8. Chapter 9 describes positive benefits (to the service provider and society as a whole) of redesigning the water tariff for the City of Kampala, Uganda, so that it is water-conserving. Finally, Chapter 10 presents progress made by Ghana Water Company Ltd to improve systems and procedures for an integrated approach to water loss management in Accra, Ghana, where non-revenue water has been estimated to be over 50%.

References

Andresen, P.P.; Lorch, R.P. and Rosegrant, M.W. (1997) *The World Food Situation: Recent Development, Emerging Issues, and Long-term Prospects*, Food Policy Report, International Food Policy Research Institute, Washington D.C.

Ellis, J.B. and Revitt, D.M. (2011) Storm water as a resource in the urban water cycle: a case study in the SWITCH demonstration of Birmingham, UK, The Future of Urban Water - Solutions for Liveable and Resilient Cities, SWITCH Conference: Paris, 24th – 26th January 2011.

Liang, X. and van Dijk, M.P. (2008) Economic and financial analysis of decentralized water recycling systems in Beijing; 3rd SWITCH Scientific Meeting: Belo Horizonte, Brazil, 30 Nov – 4 Dec, 2008.

Savenije, H. and van der Zaag, P. (2002) Water as an economic good and demand management: paradigms with pitfalls, *Water International*, 27 (1), 98-104.

Stern, N. (2007) *The Economics of Climate Change: The Stern Review*, Cambridge University Press.

Turner, A.; Willets, J.; Fane, S.; Guirco, D.; Kazaglis, A. and White, S. (2006) *Planning our future urban water resources: A guide to demand management in the context of integrated resource planning*, Institute of Sustainable Futures, University of Technology, Sydney.

UN-HABITAT (2006) *State of the world's cities*, 2006/7, UN-HABITAT, Nairobi, Kenya.

UN-HABITAT (2009) *Planning sustainable cities: global report on human settlements*, UN-HABITAT, Nairobi, Kenya.

Wenhua, J.I. and Jianming, C.A.I. (2008) Alternative water sources for agricultural production in Beijing, 3rd SWITCH Scientific Meeting: Belo Horizonte, Brazil, 30 Nov – 4 Dec 2008.

2

Introduction to Water Demand Management

Sam Kayaga

What is water demand management?

The tendency for urban water managers when faced with increased demand has previously been to plan for expanding the supply capacity to conform to the required service levels. Supply planning involves consideration of a wide range of water supply sources such as distant surface water, groundwater, desalination; as well as various sites and sizes of conventional storage, treatment and transfer options. This phenomenon is manifested in the fact that the twentieth century saw the peak of construction of big dams for water supply, and, as a result, the century was labelled the golden age of supply-side management (Allan, 2002). Increasingly, over-reliance on the development of new water supply systems to respond to increasing demand has been viewed as a potential cause of environmental degradation, hence there is a need for a general paradigm shift to consider water demand management (WDM) as well.

In most literature, WDM and water conservation have similar definitions. Other authors have differentiated between the two terminologies. Chessnutt et al (1997) define water conservation simply as reduced water use, regardless of whether the reduction in water use comes at the expense of other valued resources or unnecessarily impairs the users' life styles. Other authors such as Louw and Kassier (2002) have a restrictive definition of water conservation, to refer to efforts made to save water during situations of water shortages, usually because of drought conditions. On the other hand, Tate (1990) prefers to place water conservation in the social cost-benefit framework and defines it as the socially beneficial reduction of water use or water loss. The latter definition (Tate, 1990) emphasizes the importance of welfare benefits to the concept of water conservation, as opposed to reduction of water use per se, which is a similar concept applied by most authors to define water demand management.

There are also different definitions of WDM. Most of these definitions consider water use as a demand that can be altered through technical or non-technical interventions, unlike the traditional view of water use, which considered it as a requirement that needs to be met. One definition of WDM is '...any socially beneficial action that reduces or reschedules average or peak water withdrawals or consumption from either surface or groundwater, consistent with the protection or enhancement of water quality' (Louw and Kassier, 2002). Put in another way, WDM is any action that modifies the level and/or timing of demand for the water resource (White and Fane, 2001). As stated in Chapter 1, this guidance book adopted the definition by Savenije and van der Zaag (2002), which defined WDM as the development and implementation of strategies, policies, measures or other initiatives aimed at influencing demand, to achieve efficient and sustainable use of the scarce water resource.

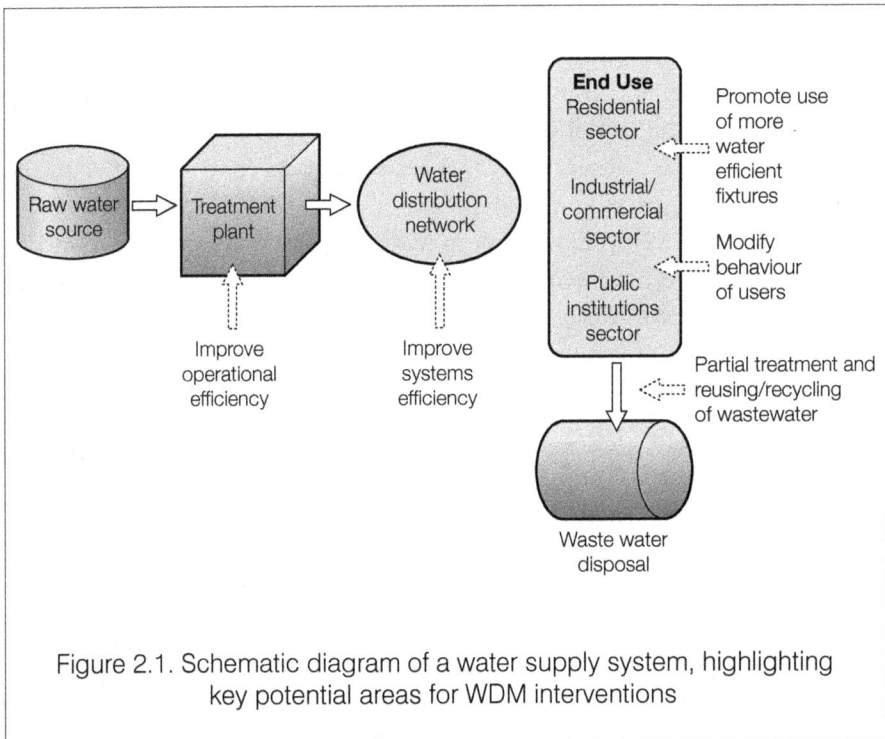

Figure 2.1. Schematic diagram of a water supply system, highlighting key potential areas for WDM interventions

Figure 2.1 shows a schematic diagram of a water supply system, highlighting potential areas for WDM intervention. It shows that WDM can be implemented through actions aimed at improving the efficiency of water treatment processes, reduction of system losses in the water distribution network, promotion of more efficient water devices and appliances in the customers' premises, and/or substitution of potable water sources. For effective WDM a water service provider should commit the necessary human, physical and material resources in actions for improving the efficiency in water use both within the water supply system and on the customers' side.

Categorizing WDM measures

There are many different WDM measures. They could be categorized in various ways, such as (Louw and Kassier, 2002):

- by type of incentive - whether through legal obligations, economic incentives, or motivated through public information/education programmes;
- by kind of tools used - structural (e.g. network improvement or retrofitting water devices in the end-users' properties), or non-structural such as pricing or education, which could lead to infrastructural improvements;
- by time horizons - whether emergency, medium or long-term measures;
- by location of the water supply systems - whether at the water treatment plant, storage tanks, conveyance and distribution network, or in the end-users' properties;
- by the entity bound to carry out the measure - e.g. the local authority, a service provider or end-users; and
- by sectors in which measures are applied, such as urban use, industrial use, or agricultural use.

For the purpose of this guidance book, WDM measures are grouped into four basic categories, i.e. structural and operational measures; economic measures; behaviour modification; legal and institutional measures. These categories are described in the following sub-sections.

Structural and operational measures

Structural measures could be taken at the utility level to reduce water losses. Examples are redesigning the water distribution network so as to carry out active leakage management, or to install pressure reducing valves in some zones identified as having unnecessarily high pressures. Structural changes could also be made in end-users' premises by replacing fixtures and appliances with devices that use water more efficiently. On the other hand, resource substitution can drastically reduce overall water consumption, especially in industries and public buildings. In that case, the plumbing system needs to be completely changed, sometimes requiring basic treatment processes to bring the water to the required water quality, so as to carry out recycling and re-use of water and wastewater.

Operational measures mainly apply to water demand management in the water distribution networks. To a smaller extent, they could apply to large consumers such as industries and public institutions. On the water service provider's side, improving operational systems and procedures for management of physical and commercial losses can go a long way to reducing water losses. Examples are capacity development of staff for effective leakage detection and repair, management and maintenance of customer meters, optimizing system pressures through efficient water pumping regimes, institutional capacity building in the utility to raise the importance of WDM measures, and ensuring accountability of staff of the water utility.

Other operational measures that a utility could introduce to enhance water demand management include universal customer metering to encourage economic usage of water; maintaining efficient and informative billing systems; detailed customer feedback systems that provide information on water use; comprehensive information, education, training and advisory services which assist customers who wish to take action to reduce their water use; provision of detailed water use analysis (audits) for water consumers in the various sectors; and financial incentives for purchase and installation of efficient water using equipment.

Economic measures

Economic measures involve '...the use of market-based signals to motivate desired types of decision-making. They either provide financial rewards for desired behaviour or impose costs for undesirable behaviour' (Cantin, Shrubsole and Ait-Ouyahia, 2005, p.2). The most commonly used economic measure is the application of volumetric-based tariff structures for customers. For the tariff to work effectively as an economic measure for WDM, customers' premises should preferably be fitted with meters that record consumption accurately, and the tariff structure should be designed so that it is water conserving. Designing a water-conserving tariff is a complex process requiring customers' social-economic data. The basic steps for designing a water-conserving tariff structure are shown in Box 1 and the concepts have been further discussed in Chapters 8 and 9 of this guidance book.

Box 1. Steps for designing a water-conserving block tariff

1. Choose a number of blocks: Conservation orientation of a tariff structure is determined by the proximity of the price of the last block to the long run marginal cost of water. The price in lower blocks usually responds to other socio-economic needs such as affordability, acceptability, political considerations and equity.
2. Choose block switch points: A conservation perspective would want to maximize the number of customers facing the appropriate price signal in the highest block. However, in practice, switch points of the blocks consider other objectives such as ensuring universal access to the lifeline supply for public health considerations.
3. Set block rates: The price in the last block should be set to the long run marginal cost of water. The price in the lower blocks will consider socio-economic needs listed above, and revenue requirements for the service provider.
4. Consider a multi-year phased approach: If conservation pricing suggests rates that are far different from existing price levels, the service provider should consider phasing the changes over multiple years.

Source: Adapted from Chesnutt et al, (2007).

Other than the tariff, a water service provider could apply subsidies to encourage water conservation by the end-users. These could be in the form of monetary and non-monetary incentives. Examples of monetary incentives are rebates on water bills and special funds for retrofitting water appliances for more efficient water use. Non-financial incentives could be in the form of call-out plumbing labour for retrofits sponsored by the water service provider or offers of sponsored water audits for end users' properties. Economic measures could also be in the form of disincentives for users who waste water, such as penalties for leakages on the customers' property.

Behaviour modification

Demand management programmes need to be designed from analysis of what motivates people to take action and change behaviour, or "social marketing". Awareness raising and public education programmes for modifying the behaviour of water consumers may be used hand in hand with other WDM measures for a more effective WDM strategy. However, public information programmes may result in short- and long-term water conservation, even though they may not be directly related to other WDM measures. To be effective, public education programmes should be planned out and implemented in a consistent and continual manner. The main objective of the programme would be to educate water users about the need to use water more efficiently in view of the overall water resources situation in the community, catchment area and globally. Another important part of the programme is to provide data and information on specific actions and measures water consumers should undertake. Informing the target audience of positive changes these actions have caused encourages greater participation in WDM programmes (Texas Water Development Board, 2004).

A variety of tools can be used to raise awareness and promote WDM programmes to the public. These include print, radio and television media; billboards, direct distribution of materials; special events such as exhibitions and tours to water supply facilities; and maintenance of an informative website. The communication tools should be tailored to the utility and the community, and where necessary, the utility should use a variety of tools, targeting different market segments. Some of the most effective public education programmes involve the participation of the consumers in the planning and implementation phase. Setting up stakeholder committees, task forces or advisory groups has been shown to be effective in defining the message and in recruiting useful allies from the communities. Partnership programmes are also effective in implementing public information programmes. Working with non-governmental organizations (NGOs) with environmental education as one of their objectives has created synergies for the service providers' public information programmes. Table 2.1 shows awareness raising and public education activities carried out in a WDM partnership programme (2006-2002) in Zaragoza, Spain, championed by Fundación Ecología y Desarrollo, an environmental NGO. Other innovative communication strategies include displaying art work portraying WDM messages in public/prominent places, periodic competitions for water efficiency ideas and games for families (Turner et al, 2003).

Table 2.1. Awareness raising and public education activities carried out in the Zaragoza WDM programme in the period 1996-2002	
Key partners	Main actions
Professionals involved in domestic water use	Project objectives and strategies mailed to builders, property agencies, promoters, architects, etc. Information sessions arranged for plumbers, distributors and manufacturers Publicity materials distributed in retail outlets Competitions organized to reward sales staff promoting water-saving devices Development & distribution of a catalogue providing water-saving technology Development & distribution of a catalogue of techniques for planning, design and maintenance of parks/gardens, and planning of water management
Large scale consumers	Information sent on environmental & economic advantages of saving water Information sessions arranged on efficient water management Stickers provided for public washrooms, which identified water-saving equipment; showed users how to use them properly; and remind users on importance of water saving
School children and teachers	Teaching materials were produced for teachers to work through with pupils: Big Book of Water - with blank pages for pupils to fill in their ideas Water Card – each pupil designed an image & slogan to persuade others of the need to preserve precious water Water Savings Book – to keep a record of monthly progressive savings achieved Experiences Directory - a collection of classroom activities related to water
General Public	Publicity campaign using TV stations, radios, newspapers, leaflets, posters, billboards, buses, urban installations. Water help-line – a telephone service to inform the public about water-saving technology and where they could find the devices. A web-page - to publicize the project on the internet Water –saving products toolkit – a package including a flow regulator for taps, water-saving shower, water-saving cistern, plus information on their use, distributed free of charge to public personalities

Source: *Fundación Ecología y Desarrollo, 2001*

School education programmes are important for influencing short- and long-term water conservation. Behavioural changes by pupils and students based on greater knowledge are often shared with adults in the household and readily implemented. For greater effectiveness, WDM concepts should be mainstreamed in the school curriculum, ensuring that the material is appropriate to the grade level of the student, increasing in complexity from elementary school through to high school. Where appropriate, the curriculum could include some practical tasks related to WDM, such as water audits, where the flow rate of faucets such as showerheads could be measured at home.

Legal and institutional measures

There is a variety of regulatory tools that can be developed to ensure uptake of WDM options. There needs to be a conducive legal and institutional framework for these tools to function effectively. There are various ways in which regulatory tools could be used to ensure efficient water use, with respect to the raw water abstraction, water distribution and end-use stages, examples of which are as shown below:

- having in place a water abstraction licensing system to ensure that abstraction of ground or surface water is environmentally and economically sustainable;

- ensuring that water service providers carry out comprehensive water resource planning to cover resource management, production management, distribution management and customer side management;

- ensuring that water service providers conform to set leakage targets, as provided for in a water act or in a performance contract;

- ensuring that water service providers have a duty to promote the efficient use of water by their consumers;

- ensuring that water service providers enforce water supply regulations for customers' properties being connected to the network to have water appliances with specified minimum water efficiency performance standards;

- ensuring that local authorities enforce building regulations for new and refurbished buildings to have water appliances and fittings with specified minimum water efficiency performance standards; and

- ensuring that industries, commercial entities, institutions and other large water consumers discharging directly into watercourses should apply for a discharge consent from the responsible regulatory agency.

Benefits and costs of implementing WDM

It is important to document the costs and benefits of WDM measures to show net benefits, and convince the relevant politicians, managers and policymakers to implement the measures. There are various difficulties in obtaining accurate cost data for many WDM measures, as they involve a bigger component of administrative or management improvement, compared to easily costed technical /technological components. However, it is important that these analyses reflect as much as possible the true capital, operation and maintenance costs associated with the WDM measures. There are three main categories in which costs and benefits may be classified: environmental, economic and social, as described in the following sub-sections.

Environmental benefits and costs

Urban water management has a significant impact on available water resources. Water withdrawals for urban services provision reduces flows in surface water bodies or ground water reservoirs in the catchment area. Today's reduction in water demand will lead to more water availability for future generations and better downstream water quality and improved water body aesthetics. Another important benefit from WDM measures is the reduction in chemicals and energy consumed for treating, transmitting and distributing water, hence resulting into reduced greenhouse gas emissions.

Potable water source substitution will also lead to less demand on the fresh water resources. Other environmental benefits of WDM specifically associated with potable water source substitution activities are that recycling/reuse of grey water and wastewater reduces the amount of pollutants being discharged in water bodies, leading to less negative environmental impacts on the ecosystem.

There are embedded environmental costs associated with the resource use for manufacturing water saving devices. Reduced wastewater flows as a result of WDM measures may also be detrimental to some members of the biodiversity. On the other hand, some activities for implementing active leakage management in water distribution networks, such as constant monitoring of pressures and flows in District Meter Areas, lead to higher greenhouse gas emissions.

Economic benefits and costs

One of the key economic benefits of implementing WDM measures in the urban water supply sector is as an alternative to augmenting the water supply and wastewater treatment infrastructure. As an example, it was estimated that the cost of obtaining additional water supply through WDM measures in South Africa would be only 20-35% of the cost of developing new water sources (Louw and Kassier, 2002). Well planned and effectively executed WDM measures on the side of the utility can reduce operation and maintenance costs (e.g. water treatment and energy pumping costs), which will result in lower tariff levels for the customers. For customers who pay their bills based on volumetric charges, water conservation activities in their premises will directly and proportionately result into reduced bills, hence freeing a portion of household income for other requirements. Furthermore, the consumer may also make a saving in terms of energy costs for water heating. Other benefits are reduction in pollution levels, and hence purification costs; and creation of jobs for those involved in implementing WDM measures.

The full economic costs of WDM measures are the sum of the full implementation costs (direct costs), the opportunity cost (i.e. the cost of foregoing the resources used for the implementation, which could have been used to carry out other economic activities), and the economic externalities exerted on other entities external to the programme (Rogers, Bhatia and Huber, 1998). Examples of direct economic costs of WDM measure are installation of water-efficient devices, maintenance and monitoring of meters, management of water leakages, education and information programmes, recycling costs and regulatory systems. Opportunity costs could be estimated as how much needs to be paid as interest charges, assuming the funds for investing in the WDM implementation programme were borrowed from a commercial bank. Externality cost varies from one context to another and an example is some people's loss of livelihoods e.g. users who may have been utilizing the water for productive uses, motivated by low tariffs. On the other hand, implementation of WDM measures could create positive externalities such as job creation in a new industry for production of water saving devices.

There is also the issue of who pays and who benefits. The capital and operating costs of augmenting water supplies are met by the utility (though these may be passed on in consumer tariffs). The capital and operating costs of some water demand measures however may be met directly by the consumer, for example the cost of a water-efficient toilet or washing machine, or the costs of storage (and possibly pumping) to reuse rainwater or grey water. Economic instruments may be used as discussed in Chapter 8 to encourage water consumers to adopt water-saving measures and/or subsidize the costs of the water saving devices.

Social benefits and costs

Estimating social benefits and costs related to WDM measures is more difficult than for economic considerations. Yet having a change in the quantity of water supplied may have far-reaching consequences for the users, both directly and in form of externalities. It is important that WDM strategies take into consideration the interests of the most vulnerable in society, such as poor households, and the women, who often obtain lifeline water supplies at a high personal or social cost. The vulnerable usually have less influence and voice, and tend to get no priority in the provision of infrastructure services. Water consumption for such vulnerable groups should not be reduced to a level that is below the socially desirable threshold. WDM strategies can deliberately be designed with one of the objectives being to enhance social equity. The direct social benefits for the vulnerable in society may be through improved access as a result of implementation of a water conserving tariff that is also socially equitable. On the other hand, the vulnerable in society may benefit indirectly through implementation of water-conserving tariffs that lead to improved service coverage, which in turn enable the poor to obtain water from the piped water system at a lower cost, compared to what they may be currently paying to small-scale service providers.

If well planned and implemented, WDM measures will make water more affordable to the vulnerable in society, often the poor. Communities may be more informed, and therefore empowered. WDM measures may also create job opportunities for members of the community, such as carrying out water audits, retrofitting and manufacturing water efficient devices. WDM measures will reduce the costs to society, by extending the life of existing water supplies, and lead to sustainability of water service provision. Wastewater flows will be reduced, and there will be energy savings for members of the household who use less water. On the whole, WDM will lead to less pollution of the environment, and therefore reduce the cleaning-up costs incurred by society.

There will also be a social cost that members of society have to pay for effective implementation of WDM measures. The most common economic measure is to raise the water tariffs, and so most members of the community may have to pay more for water services. End-users may have to buy and install efficient water devices, which is an extra cost to the customers. For some consumers, they may have to change their lifestyles to use less water, which may come with a social cost.

Examples of WDM in practice

Many WDM interventions may be going on in different parts of the world, but not all of them are reported in the public domain. This section cites a few examples of documented good practices in implementation of WDM. An evaluation study of Australia's Sydney Water Corporation 'Every Drop Counts' residential retrofit programme (2000-2002) showed that a single participating household saved about 20 m^3 per year, equating to about

4.18 million m³ per year for the 200,000 houses that participated in the programme (Turner et al, 2005). In the commercial sector, case studies carried out on two commercial high-rise buildings in Melbourne and Sydney showed that reductions of up to 80% of the scheme water demand and 90% of sewage discharge can be achieved through the integration of innovative water efficiency measures, rainfall harvesting, treated effluent reuse, and evapotranspiration through roof gardens (Chanan et al, 2003).

Wintgens et al (2005) report on several case studies worldwide where various advanced treatment processes such as microfiltration, utrafiltration, nanofiltration, reverse osmosis, ozonation, and/or ultraviolet disinfection have been used for reclamation and reuse of municipal wastewater. Cases include (i) the water reclamation and management scheme at Sydney Olympic Park where 2,000 m³/per day of combined domestic sewage and storm water is treated and then distributed through a separate pipe network; (ii) an advanced treatment plant in Wollongong, Australia is treating 20,000 m³/day of low-nutrient tertiary effluent; (iii) 2,500,000 m³/year of effluent from the wastewater treatment plants in Wulpen, Belgium is treated and then infiltrated in the dunes on the Flemish coast of Belgium; (iv) an advanced water treatment plant reclaims 70 million gallons per day of clarified secondary treatment in Orange State California which is then used for groundwater recharge and for a seawater intrusion barrier; (v) 21,000 m³/day of secondary effluent from a municipal wastewater treatment plant in Windhoek, Namibia is reclaimed, treated to drinking water quality level by a complex treatment train, and then distributed for direct potable reuse; and (vi) the NEWater project in Singapore was reclaiming about 91,000 m³/day as of January 2004 to supplement freshwater raw resources. A few other examples are summarized in Table 2.2.

Table 2.2. Examples of benefits of DM as reported in the literature

Study Reference	Study setting	Action	Achievement
Martindale & Gleick, 2001	New York, USA	City Council provided rebates for installing low-volume water closets	Reduction in overall household use by 29%
Gumbo, 2004 & Mkandla, Van der Zaag and Sibanda, 2005	Bulawayo, Zimbabwe	Public education and rationing	Reduction of consumption by 25%
Smith et al, 2001	Millennium Dome London	Use of a combination of poor ground water, grey water and rainwater for toilet flushing	Savings of about 50% of potable water consumption
Ahn & Song, 2000	Lotte World, Seoul, South Korea	Reclamation of wastewater for toilet flushing	18% (900m³/day) of total water supply provided
Holt, Phillips & Bates, 2000	Three UK industries	Installing water-efficient devices & new technology	30% reduction in water consumption
Yeoh et al, 2001	Malaysia	Reusing the spent wash in molasses dilution and fermentation	40% reduction in freshwater consumption
March et al, 2004	Mallorca Island, Spain	Recycling of grey water to flush toilets at a local hotel	23% of water consumption was saved

References

Ahn, K.H. and Song, K.G. (2000) Application of micro-filtration with a novel fouling control method for reuse of wastewater from a large-scale resort complex. *Desalination*, 129(3), 207-216.

Allan, J.A. (2002) *The Middle East water question: hydropolitics and the global economy*, I.B. Tauris & Co. Ltd, London.

Cantin, B. Shrubsole, D. and Ait-Ouyahia, M. (2005) Using economic instruments for water demand management: introduction, *Canadian Water Resources Journal*, 30(1), 1-10.

Chanan, V., White, S., Howe, C. and Jha, M. (2003) Sustainable water management in commercial office buildings,in: *Innovation in Water: Ozwater Convention and Exhibition, 6-10 April 2003, Perth, Australia.*

Chesnutt, T.W.; Beecher, J.A. Mann, P.C. Michael Hanemann, W. Raftelis, G.A. McSpadden, C.N. Pekelney, D.M. Christianson, J. and Krop, R. (1997) *Designing, evaluating and implementing conservation rate structures*, The California Urban Water Conservation Council, USA.

Fundación Ecología y Desarrollo (2001) *Zaragoza, saving water city – 50 best practices*, unpublished report, Zaragoza, Spain.

Gumbo, B., (2004) The status of water demand management in selected cities of southern Africa, *Physics and Chemistry of the Earth*, 29 15/18),.1225–1231

Holt , C.P.; Phillips, P.S. and Bates, M.P. (2000) Analysis of the role of waste minimisation clubs in reducing industrial water demand in the UK, *Resources, Conservation and Recycling*, 30 (4), 315–331.

Louw, D.B. and Kassier, W.E. (2002) *The costs and benefits of water demand management*, Centre for International Agricultural Marketing and Development (CIAMD), Paarl, South Africa.

March, J.G.; Gual, M. and Orozco, F. (2004) Experiences on greywater re-use for toilet flushing in a hotel (Mallorca Island, Spain) *Desalination*, 164(3), 241-247.

Martindale, D., Gleick, P.H. (2001) How we can do it? *Scientific American* (February 18,2001)).

Mkandla N., Van der Zaag P. and Sibanda P. (2005) Bulawayo water supplies: Sustainable alternatives for the next decade, *Physics and Chemistry of the Earth*, 30(11-16), 935–942.

Rogers, P.; Bhatia, R. and Huber, A. (1998) *Water as a social and economic good: how to put the principle in practice.* (Technical Advisory Committee Background Paper No. 2), Global Water Partnership, Stockholm, Sweden.

Savenije, H. and van der Zaag, P. (2002) Water as an economic good and demand management: paradigms with pitfalls, *Water International*, 27 (1), 98-104.

Smith, A.J.; Khowa, J.; Lodgea, B. and Bavister, G (2001) Desalination of poor quality brackish groundwater for non-potable use, *Desalination*, 139(1-3), 207–215.

Tate, D.M. (1990) *Water demand management in Canada: a state-of-the-art review*, (Social Science Series No. 23), Inland Waters Directorate, Ottawa, Canada.

Texas Water Development Board (2004) *Water Conservation Best Management Practice (BMP) Guide*, (Report No. 362), Water Conservation Implementation Task Force, Texas.

Turner, A. Campbell, S.; White, S. and Milne, G. (2003) *Alice Springs Water Efficiency Study, Stage 1 and 2 Final Report, Volume 1*, Institute for Sustainable Futures, University of Technology, Sydney, Australia.

Turner, A.; White, S.; Beatty, K. and Gregory, A. (2005) Results of the largest residential demand management programme in Australia,in: *International IWA conference on the Efficient Water Use and Management of Urban Water, Santiago, Chile, 15-15 March 2005*.

Wintgens, T.; Melin, T.; Schafer, A.; Khan, S.; Muston, M.; Bixio, D. and Theoye, C. (2005) The role of membrane processes in municipal wastewater reclamation and reuse, *Desalination*, 178, 1-11.

White, S.B. and Fane, S.A. (2001) Designing cost effective water demand management programs in Australia, *Water Science and Technology*, 46(6-7),p.225-232.

Yeoh, B.G.; Chen, S.S.; Aziz, A.A.; Nee, T.Y.; Chong, T.C.; van de Graff, R. and van de Graff, H. (2001) Cleaner production in distillery industry - the Malaysia experience, in: *Proceedings of the Third Asia Pacific Roundtable Conference for Cleaner Production. 28 February - 2 March, 2001 Manila, Philippines*.

Zaragoza Ayuntamiento (AYTO) (2009) *Zaragoza in SWITCH Project*, unpublished report, Zaragoza, Spain.

3

Integrated Resource Planning Approach

Sam Kayaga and Ian Smout

Need for a paradigm shift

Water sector professionals face daunting challenges to meet global water needs in an environmentally sustainable manner, amidst the increasing population coupled with impacts of climate change on the water resources. As discussed in Chapter 1, the situation is more critical in urban areas of developing countries where populations are escalating at an alarming rate. The current conventional urban water management concept, which was developed in the 19th century mainly to counter epidemics caused by water-borne pathogens, cannot adequately respond to these challenges. Under this conventional system, the design for the urban water infrastructure services was mainly driven by public health considerations, rather than environmental sustainability. Understandably, this did not take due consideration of the rapid population growth rates, high levels of urbanization, industrial growth and climate change, which the world is currently experiencing.

A key limitation of the conventional urban water system is the use of high quality drinking water for all domestic purposes. Yet, there are substantial differences in water quality demanded for different uses in the household. Only drinking and cooking, which consume a small proportion of the total household demand, require high quality treated water. Other uses may be satisfied with poorer quality water, which could permit re-use of water from one application to another. Use of such high quality water for all household chores has implications on the production costs and the unnecessarily higher pollution loads arising out of the treatment processes (SWITCH 2010a).

Furthermore, large volumes of drinking water are used to transport excreta over long distances to centralized wastewater treatment plants. Limitations of such a sewerage system are: (i) the capacity of the centralized end-of-pipe treatment processes to absorb large volumes of wastes and effluents are being stretched to their limits, (ii) valuable resources in terms of potable water and nutrients are wasted during the transportation and treatment processes; (iii) extensive sewer networks are costly and difficult to construct and maintain; and (iv) performance of large-scale treatment facilities is reduced under wet weather conditions, when wastewater is heavily diluted (*ibid*).

Another key limitation of the conventional urban water management concept is over-emphasis on managing supply at the expense of considering demand options. The traditional response to the ever increasing water demand is development of new water sources. Such supply management tendencies are neither environmentally sustainable nor economically viable, as they lead to higher rates of depletion of the finite water resources at higher marginal costs.

Under conventional urban water management systems, the institutional setup engenders a highly fragmented division of responsibilities and tasks. In many cases, different organizations do not share information, and activities in the catchment areas are not coordinated. Urban water managers in water supply, sanitation and drainage have largely been working in isolation, focusing on their individual sectors. As a result, many urban water managers do not fully appreciate the impact their operations have on the environment, and environmental sustainability is rarely part of the corporate objectives. Where there are efforts to mitigate against environmental degradation, the efforts are mostly ad hoc, and often fragmented.

Clearly, conventional approaches to urban water management cannot meet the growing global needs and at the same time sustain the environment. A new paradigm is needed. In addition to technical advances such as advanced water treatment processes, the new paradigm must also address a multiplicity of issues such as those concerned with socio-cultural, technological, financial, economic, gender, institutional, political and environmental aspects (Grigg, 1998). This means that water authorities must transform into 'water service providers', developing their expertise in multiple fields such as engineering and new technologies, environmental and social sciences, economics, marketing, policy, customer care, health, consultation and applied research (Turner et al, 2006). Integrated Resource

Planning has been adopted since the early 1990s by service water providers in various parts of the world as a best practice planning framework that fulfils these requirements.

What is integrated resource planning?

The Integrated Resource Planning (IRP) approach originated in the energy sector, primarily as a response to dramatic oil price increases of the 1970s. At the time, the energy sector recognized that traditional planning approaches focused only on construction of energy supply infrastructure, which was not only capital-intensive, but consumption of the energy supplied led to pervasive externalities, ranging from local pollution and global greenhouse gases, to energy and nuclear security risks, which are normally not considered in the energy supply costing (Swisher, Jannuzzi and Redlinger, 1997). Initially, IRP was used as a planning and policy framework to develop energy efficiency initiatives, to respond to the aforementioned issues. During the 1990s, water sector professionals in various parts of the world adapted this framework to carry out resource planning for the water sector.

Applied to the water sector, IRP may be defined as a comprehensive form of planning that uses an open and participatory decision-making process to evaluate least-cost analyses of demand-side and supply side options, which are assessed against a common set of planning objectives or criteria (Beecher, 1995; Swisher, Jannuzzi and Redlinger, 1997; Tellus Institute, 2000). The guiding philosophy for IRP is that utility customers do not necessarily demand for a resource itself but rather for the services that the resource provides, often called end uses (Fane, Turner and Mitchell, 2004). Therefore, in the IRP framework, water utilities determine the least cost options that they can use to provide their customers with water-related services that they demand rather than the water per se (Howe and White, 1999). In their definitions, Maddaus and Maddaus (2001) and Sharifi (2003) also emphasize open and participatory decision-making processes involving all stakeholders; consideration of a community's quality of life; environmental issues that may be impacted by the ultimate decision; and recognition of the multiple and competing uses of water.

Applying one of IRP's key guiding principles, customers should be perceived as having demand for the end uses, such as clothes washing or toilet flushing, rather than a demand for litres of water (White and Fane, 2001). Since customers of water utilities require services rather water quantity per se, water supply systems should be designed and managed to satisfy water-related service needs or end-uses. Key characteristics that distinguish IRP from the traditional planning processes are highlighted in Table 3.1.

Table 3.1. Comparison of traditional urban planning with IRP		
CRITERIA:	Traditional Planning	IRP
Planning Orientation		
Resource options	Supply options with little diversity	Supply and demand management options; efficiency and diversity are encouraged
Resource ownership and control	Utility-owned and centralized	Some resources owned by other utilities, other producers, customers
Scope of planning	Single objective, usually to add to supply capacity	Multiple objectives determined in the planning process
Assessment criteria	Maximize reliability and minimise costs	Multiple criteria, including cost control, risk management, environmental protection, economic development
Resource selection	Based on a commitment to a specific option	Based on developing a mix of options
Planning Process		
Nature of the process	Closed, inflexible, internally oriented	Open, flexible, externally oriented
Judgement and preferences	Implicit	Explicit
Conflict management	Conventional dispute resolution	Consensus-building
Stakeholders	Utility staff and its rate-payers	Multiple interests
Role of stakeholders	Disputants	Participants
Planning Issues		
Supply reliability	Constraint and high priority	A decision variable
Environmental quality	A planning constraint, comply with regulations	A planning objective
Cost considerations	Direct utility system costs	Direct and indirect costs, including environmental & social externalities
Role of pricing	A mechanism to recover costs	An economic signal to guide consumption, and a way for sharing costs and benefits between different stakeholders
Risk and uncertainty	Should be avoided or reduced	Should be analysed and managed

Source: Turner el al, 2006

Table 3.1 shows glaring differences between the two planning approaches, such that changing from a conventional urban water planning process to IRP requires a complete reorientation. The key principles of IRP that need to be embraced are (Turner et al, 2006):

- the recognition that it is the service that is required by customers and not the water itself,

- the need to carry out detailed demand forecasting – dis-aggregation of demand into end uses such as toilets and showers enables detailed demand forecasting as well as determining the potential of water conservation with respect to various options,

- consideration of a broad spectrum of viable options that satisfy service needs,

- comparison of options using a common metric, boundary and assumptions,

- the importance of participatory process, which ensures that diverse groups of stakeholders are involved at different stages of the planning process, and therefore identify and respond to multiple needs and objectives, and

- using adaptive management – emphasis on iterative, on-going learning process in which initiatives are decided upon, implemented and evaluated in repeated cycles.

IRP thus provides a framework for analysing water demand management options and comparing these with alternative urban water management options, for example augmented supplies. IRP has a broader scope than WDM, but in this book we focus on how IRP provides a systematic approach to WDM.

IRP concepts have been applied in various contexts by water utilities around the world, with significant work done in America and Australia. In the US, the leaders in this field have been California Urban Conservation Council and the American Water Works Association, and their focus has been mainly the demand side. More recently, the Institute of Sustainable Futures (ISF), a research institute of the University of Technology, Sydney has been at the forefront of applying IRP principles in Australia. ISF has worked with various water utilities in Australia to develop a coherent integrated process that brings together essential IRP elements to ' …unlock the potential in DM and compare water conservation options on equal footing with source substitution and supply options' (Mitchell et al, 2004, p.4). The IRP process undertaken by ISF in Australian cities, described on page 32 may be adapted for other settings, such as the example of strategic planning for WDM in Alexandria described on page 54.

Multi-stakeholder planning for urban water management

As shown in Table 3.1, the IRP approach includes participation of stakeholders in planning, through seeking consensus. The SWITCH project adopted this approach through the development of "Learning Alliances" and Strategic Planning processes. A Learning Alliance is a group of stakeholder organisations that seeks to create change and widespread impact. The development of Learning Alliances in the SWITCH cities was based on the following reasoning (Butterworth et al. 2011):

- Complex problems, like urban water management and its governance, require creative solutions and a group of multi-disciplinary stakeholders working interactively are likely to come up with better options than an individual organisation with command and control authority;

- Putting research into use and scaling up innovation requires key stakeholders to focus on this issue and develop agreed strategies; and

- Good governance – transparent decision making and accountability – can be promoted through Learning Alliances of stakeholders.

Learning Alliances were supported by facilitators and researchers in the SWITCH cities, to undertake a range of activities as shown in Box 3.1. These include visioning, scenario building and strategy development, as show in Figure 3.1.

Under this multi-stakeholder strategic planning process, options are considered for achieving the desired end vision, under various possible future scenarios. This includes demand management options covering end use water conservation, water loss management, source substitution etc, as well as options for augmenting water supply. As discussed in later sections of this chapter, analysis of these options is a major challenge. The IRP approach considers multiple objectives and criteria, including a common metric of cost per unit of water saved or delivered, risk management, environmental protection, economic development and social issues. The SWITCH Project found that Learning Alliances of stakeholders working together can be effective in encouraging a broad, long term perspective, beyond the limited time scales and responsibilities of individual organisations.

Box 3.1. Typical SWITCH Learning Alliance activities

- Meetings: very many and with different purposes, including bilateral meetings focused on developing trust, understanding and gaining buy-in of various key stakeholders
- Workshops on various topics such as interesting technologies or approaches, visioning and scenario-based joint planning and strategy development
- Training aiming to build awareness and skills of best practice of city practitioners (in subjects like demand management)
- Facilitating communications on the activities of SWITCH and other related actors in the city e.g. using e-mail groups and newsletters (printed or electronic)
- Needs assessment and expressing demand for research or other interventions based on a shared understanding of real underlying local problems
- Design of pilot demonstration projects (in local partnerships) to test new technologies and approaches
- Awareness raising activities e.g. engagement of local mass media, school art competitions, and joining other city initiatives
- Visits to other cities and key sector events
- Process documentation: documenting what happens but also why things happen (or don't)

Source: Butterworth (2009)

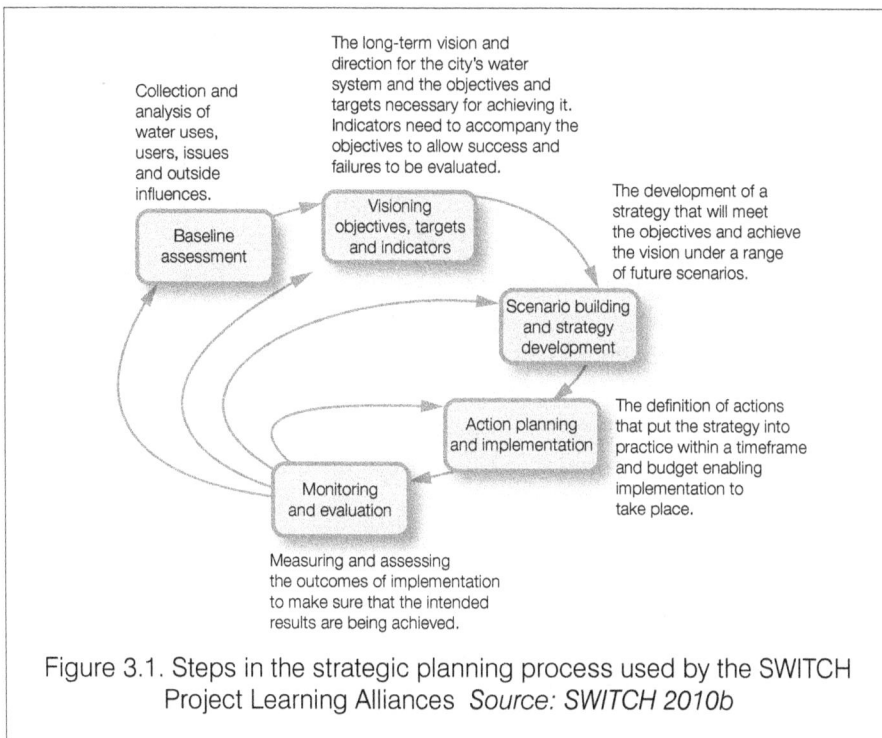

Figure 3.1. Steps in the strategic planning process used by the SWITCH Project Learning Alliances *Source: SWITCH 2010b*

Planning also requires the use of models to examine the consequences of different scenarios, and decision support tools to analyse the data in terms of key indicators. Within the SWITCH Project the CITY WATER knowledge management and decision support system (Mackay and Last, 2010) was developed for compiling available data related to all aspects of urban water management, and analysing alternatives in terms of indicators like water requirements, energy demands, water quality, financial costs and cost recovery. SWITCH also developed models for specific tasks in water demand management, as described in chapters 4, 5 and 6. In particular, the Water Demand Management Options model (chapter 4) is based on an IRP approach.

The IRP framework applied in Australia

Since the mid 1990s, ISF has championed the implementation of IRP by various water service providers in Australia. Notable examples include (i) a domestic water efficiency programme for 30,000 people by Water Corporation of Western Australia in 1995 (Botica and White, 1996); (ii) residential and non-residential water efficiency programmes implemented by Sydney Water Corporation in 1997/98, and subsequently evaluated (Howe and White, 1999; Turner et al, 2005); (iii) the Alice Springs water efficiency study (Turner el al, 2003); and the sector-based analysis and options model development in Canberra (Turner, White and Bickford, 2005). Figure 3.2 shows a process diagram that has been applied for urban water systems in Australia and has been continuously refined by ISF. The following sub-sections, which are mainly based on materials from Turner et al (2006) and Mitchell et al (2004) describe in detail the steps undertaken in the ISF process.

Planning for the overall process

Before getting deeply into the IRP process, it is important to spend time thinking through the whole process and producing a clear plan of action for the participants and engender ownership of the process by the multiple stakeholders. Members of the planning team not conversant with IRP concepts should be initiated into the process, clearly differentiating it from the traditional planning approaches, and getting to appreciate its scope. A WDM programme must respond to local conditions, and so it is necessary to identify the local drivers for the IRP process, which will influence how the planning process is followed. The drivers could be categorized as direct (such as supply gap due to an increasing population); indirect (such as implications of climate change on catchment runoff); or organizational

Data Collection

- ABS
- Other Government Statistics

- Questionnaires
- Surveys
- Data Loggers
- Other studies

Water service provider

Surveys

Demographic data

Stock data

End user data

Bulk water

Metered water

Other water sources

End use model

Demand Forecasting:
Residential
- End use analysis
Non-residential
- Historical/future trends, sector analysis
Unaccounted for water
- Historical/future trends

Options model

Options analysis:
a) Develop options (including demand management, source substitution, reuse, and new potable supplies)
b) Assess options (using LCP to compare unit cost of each option in terms of: '$/ML water provided/saved')
c) Identify investment order of options (ordered suite of preferred options, starting with lowest unit cost)

Further focused data collection
- Pilot studies
- Experiments
- Surveys

Program implementation plan

Implementation

Interim evaluation

Adaptive management response

Overall program evaluation:
- Surveys
- Meter readings
- Data loggers (flow trace analysis)

Climate correction model

Key:

Data

Process step

Model

ABS: Australian Bureau of Statistics   LCP: Least Cost Planning

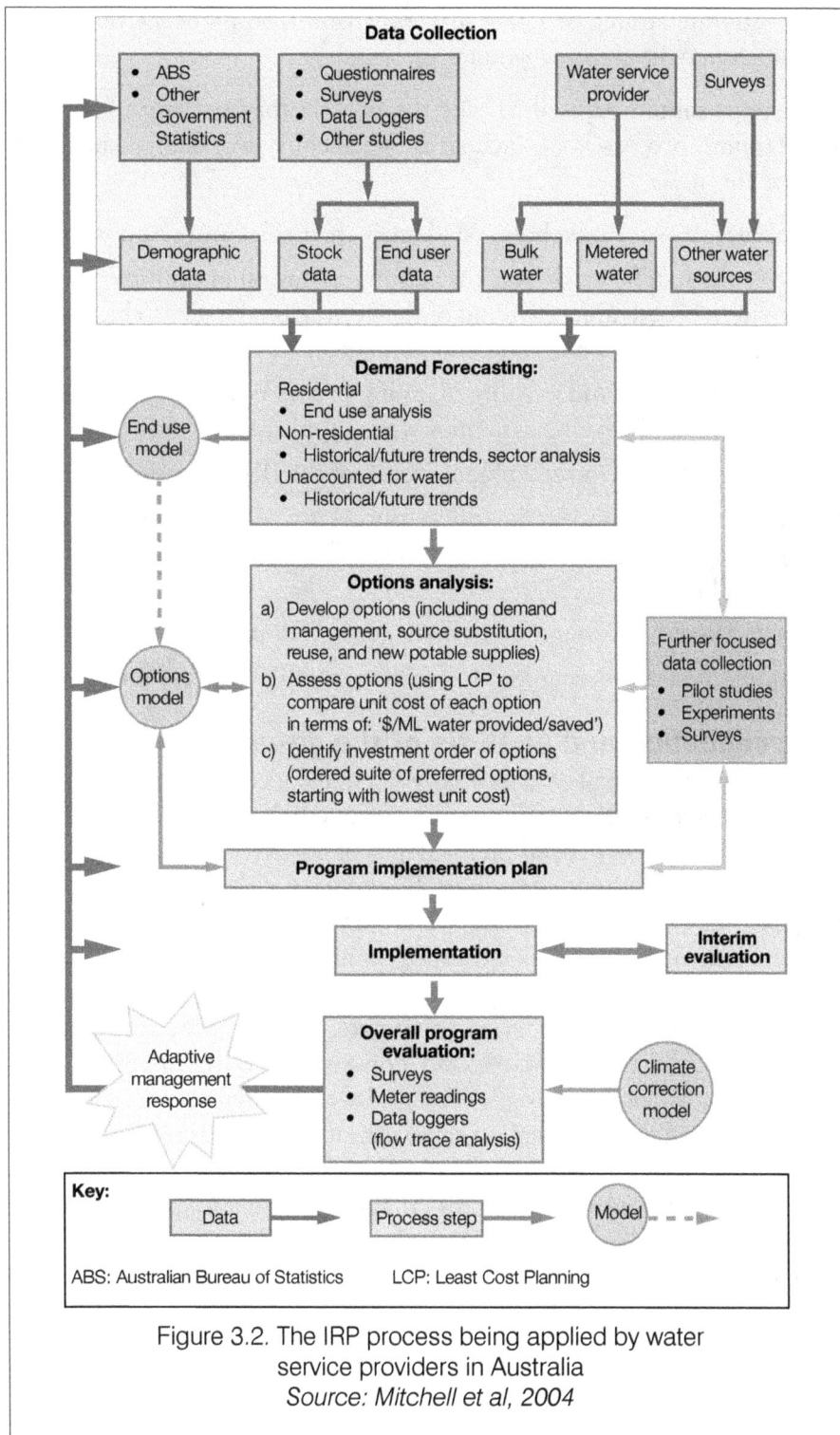

Figure 3.2. The IRP process being applied by water service providers in Australia
Source: Mitchell et al, 2004

(e.g. corporate strategy). These drivers will in turn influence the targets set, which may be short-, medium- or long-term.

Workshops should be used to take the process forward and ensure that the planning process is all-inclusive. Specifically, workshops should be utilized to:

- mobilize relevant stakeholders; identify their roles and responsibilities,
- define the significant drivers for action - inclusion of multiple views to provide a broad understanding of the key regional issues to be resolved by water resources planning and management;
- identify previous and existing planning processes being undertaken in the region, and develop synergies where applicable;
- develop and agree a preliminary vision of the IRP process;
- determine available funds and resources to be provided by various organizations, and obtain commitment from all parties to fulfil their responsibilities;
- define a steering committee to manage the IRP process; and
- identify documents required to facilitate the IRP process review.

Data collection and analysis of the situation

The next step is to collect data that will enable identification of regional issues and determination of the supply-demand balance. The level of detail of data collected will depend on the depth of the investigation. A decision needs to be made about the system boundary for the planning process. Examples of boundaries are the water supply service area, wastewater service area, or a geographical/topographical boundary that includes storm water runoff characteristics of the region. Every region will have different characteristics in terms of climate, demographic and land use characteristics, existing potable and non-potable water supply sources and systems, water using appliances, and water usage practices in terms of customer behaviour. Based on these characteristics, factors influencing both supply yield and demand can then be worked out. Figure 3.3 shows an example of a flowchart of factors that could influence demand. Based on preliminary information, and before detailed data collection, the team, through a participatory process, should conduct a 'first-cut' identification of issues, risks and opportunities for effective water resources management in the region.

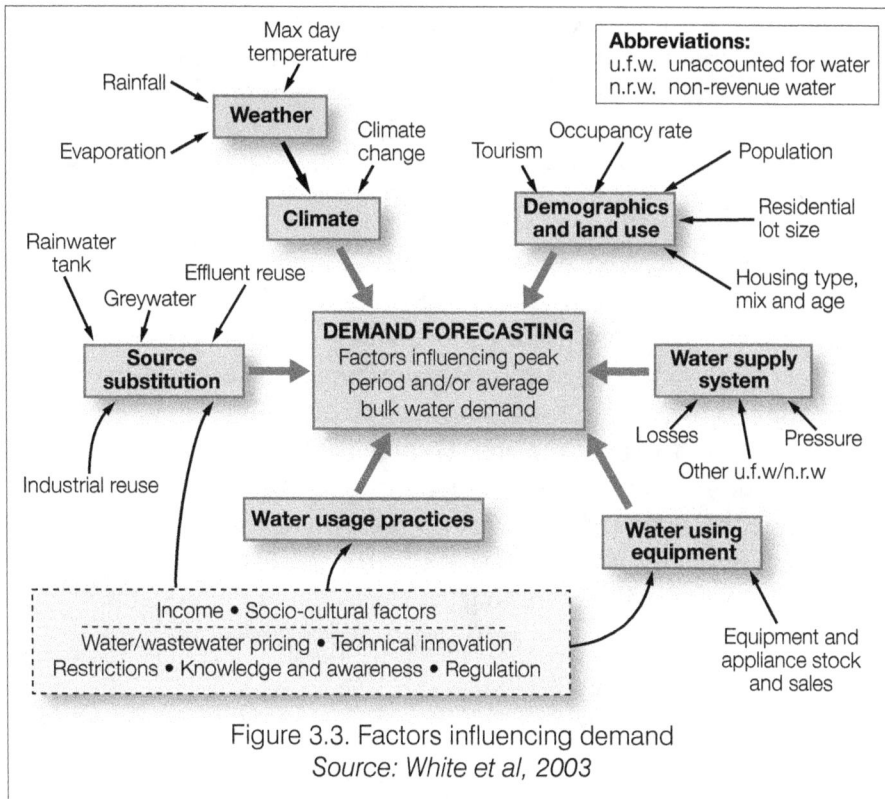

Abbreviations:
u.f.w. unaccounted for water
n.r.w. non-revenue water

Max day temperature

Rainfall

Weather

Climate change

Evaporation

Climate

Occupancy rate

Tourism

Population

Demographics and land use

Residential lot size

Rainwater tank

Effluent reuse

Greywater

Housing type, mix and age

Source substitution

DEMAND FORECASTING
Factors influencing peak period and/or average bulk water demand

Water supply system

Losses

Pressure

Other u.f.w/n.r.w

Industrial reuse

Water usage practices

Water using equipment

Income • Socio-cultural factors
Water/wastewater pricing • Technical innovation
Restrictions • Knowledge and awareness • Regulation

Equipment and appliance stock and sales

Figure 3.3. Factors influencing demand
Source: White et al, 2003

After getting a feel of the specific issues, risks and opportunities in the region, the next step is to investigate in greater depth the supply-demand balance. There is need to forecast the demand accurately, and it is recommended that instead of using the traditional historical forecasting based on per capita demand, a bottom-up approach of end-use analysis for residential demand is used. This is a method where the demand in a household is disaggregated into specific indoor end uses (such as toilets, showers, washing machine) and outdoor end uses (such as garden watering, car washing, and swimming pools). Demand forecasting is better done through modelling. The choice of model for arriving at the demand forecast will dictate the scope and form of data needs.

For detailed analysis, the model requires more in-depth end-use data to be collected, in addition to the generic demographic/socio-economic data such as population growth rates, house types, and occupancy ratios. The model will also require utility-side data such as customer-metered data, sector-disaggregated water demand and information relating to management of non-revenue water. The analysis also utilises (secondary) historical data, such as those obtained through regression analysis, used for establishing an empirical relationship between historical water demand and key variables such as maximum daily temperatures, rainfall, evaporation, land use change, household income, household size, and water tariffs. Table 3.2 shows data requirements for the end use model for South Australian Water Company in 2007.

When the relevant data have been collected, a sector-based demand forecast for a long-term period (e.g. 50 years) can be carried out as an initial step leading to the more detailed end-use demand forecast. Depending on data availability, the sector-based forecast may be combined with the supply yield calculations, and the gap between supply and demand may be identified for each year over a specific time period. Various assumptions may be made, for instance in connection with the yield or population growth rate, so as to arrive at various risk scenarios. This analysis will produce a reference case, in which the water demand is projected under a 'business as usual' or 'do nothing' situation.

For the bottom-up end-use analysis, more detailed primary data may need to be collected from the consumers. These data are specific to the region and may be collected through various methods (Cordell, Robson and Loh, 1993), such as metering, data logging, consumer diaries and/or surveys. The surveys could be face-to-face doorstep, face-to-face in-house, technical inspection, telephone, or market surveys. Each of the methods has advantages and disadvantages, and using a combination of methods is recommended. End-use data collection aims to establish what type of appliances are being used in the customers' premises, how much water is used each time, and how often are they used. Data are also collected regarding outdoor end uses. Box 3.2 shows typical end uses researched in Australia. Another category of data that is important is what the stock of various water appliances is in a given location, and how it is likely to change over time. This information is necessary for forecasting demand and determining potential savings from water efficiency programmes.

Table 3.2. Data requirements for IRP process for South Australian Water Company	
Bulk water demand	Reservoir corrected daily bulk water demand for the last 10 to 20 years (and aggregated into months and quarters if available).
Customer potable metered demand	Metered demand, single residential, multi residential (per unit of occupancy not just property), commercial, industrial, institutional
	Greater split by customer type over same period if possible for interested customers Commercial/industrial (e.g. hotels) and say top 150 water using customers Institutional (e.g. schools, hospital, government buildings, outdoor parks)
	No. of customers/properties in each identified sector and customer type over same time period.
Non potable demand	Same kind of information for non potable demand
	Other non potable demand such as bores and rainwater tanks
Non revenue water (NRW)	Any official calculations used to assess the non revenue water component of demand
Population	Population catered for since the early 1990s (pop, households, occupancy ratio)
	Population projections (pop, households, occupancy ratio)
Land planning	Any specific information on planned development and trends in recent development in residential and non residential sectors
Sewage	Total sewage flows over the same period in days/months/quarters as is available
	Sewage discharge factors
Service area	Area serviced by water and wastewater
Maps	Maps of service area (including zones)
Climate	Rainfall, evaporation and temperature
Influences on demand	Timing and levels of restrictions through the 90s and since 2000 and who affected (e.g. residential/non residential).
	The demand management programmes that have been implemented over the same period and the participants each month/quarter (whatever detail you collate)
	Price modifications (water and wastewater) over the same period. A table of dates and price (including fixed component) would be good.
	Leakage and pressure reduction programs for your system.
End uses	Information on the number of efficient/non efficient toilets, showers etc. in the area
Other information	Strategic documents
	Yield information
	Demand options
	Supply options
	Marginal cost of water

Source: Turner & White, 2003

INDOOR END USES	OUTDOOR END USES
Toilet	Pool/spa
Bath	Irrigation systems
Shower	Evaporative air conditioners
Wash basin	Lawn/garden
Washing machine	Car washing
Laundry tap	
Kitchen tap	
Dishwasher	

Source: Turner et al, 2006

After analysing the supply-demand gap in the region more accurately, the reference stakeholder group can then have a more focused discussion on the water resources management in the region, leading to a reassessment of issues, risks and opportunities. The estimations and assumptions made in the demand-supply forecasts must be fully explained to the stakeholders, during the reassessment of priorities in the region. The risks and uncertainties should be well discussed, to ensure and maintain transparency of the IRP process. After going through the reassessment process carefully and thoroughly, the planning objectives may then be set, through a well defined process of engagement and participation. The planning objectives should be clear and well aligned with agreed priorities of the region. These objectives should be easily measurable, so that progress can be monitored/evaluated, and should have minimal conflict with other objectives set in the region.

Development of the response

The planning objectives arrived at in the previous step should be appropriately framed, so that they align to the perspective of possible responses in the given context. It should then be decided what level of analysis of options of costs and benefits will be undertaken, in line with the planning objectives. A common output of an IRP process is a suite of WDM options, which will best meet the long-term requirement for balancing supply and demand, at the lowest cost to society. The depth of analysis could be detailed or first-cut, full or partial. The analysis will lead to identification and design of potential options for effective management of the supply-demand gap. Alternatively, with availability of data, supply-side options may also be developed with the demand-side options so that all the options maybe compared with each other. Table 3.3 shows factors and/or policy actions that influence supply or demand.

In order to target WDM options more accurately and effectively, there is need to disaggregate the current water demand of homogeneous consumer categories into sectors and subsectors. Demand may be categorised into three main sectors: residential, non-residential and non-revenue water. Residential demand may further be subdivided into single residential or multi-residential; non-residential demand could be industrial, commercial or public institutional (e.g. hospitals, schools, public recreational); and non-revenue water could be predominantly physical losses or commercial losses. Initially, opportunities for enhanced water conservation could be sought for current water demand in these sectors and sub-sectors, giving consideration of contemporary trends in the region, such as high growth of tourism, increasing industrial activities, expansion of multi-residential block apartments and high levels of non-revenue water.

Table 3.3. Factors or policy actions that influence yield or demand, as considered in Australia	
Supply-side options	Demand side options
New dams, pipelines, groundwater, desalination	Improve system efficiency (e.g. leakage, pressure management)
Changed environmental flow regime	Improve water-use market • metering, billing and pricing • education and advisory services
Reuse schemes for environmental flows	Improve residential water use efficiency (incentives, retrofit, regulation) • appliances and fixtures • landscapes and irrigation
Indirect potable reuse into storage	Improve business water efficiency (incentives, retrofit, regulation)
Changed drought response strategies: • restricted regime • emergency supply readiness • drought pricing	Substitute potable use (on-site or larger scale) • rain tanks and storm water • grey water and effluent reuse • groundwater

Source: Turner et al, 2006

After considering generic WDM options according to sectors and sub-sectors, the next step is to analyse responses that promote higher efficiency levels of the stock of water appliances and devices, as well as targeting their usage times. Water demand disaggregated according to the stock of appliances can better enable the water service provider to determine where potential exists for maximising water conservation by converting existing appliances to more efficient ones, where applicable. End uses are commonly homogeneous in the residential sector, and so identifying the conservation potential may be easily accomplished. It may be more difficult to consider conservation potential for some categories of the non-residential sector where the end uses are less homogeneous. For the non-homogeneous categories, case-by-case in-depth studies may be the most accurate source of required data. For water distribution network, application of the performance measures recommended by the International Water Association (IWA) will provide a good indication of the water conservation potential.

Only a small fraction of the water used in households and many other non-residential applications needs to be of high bacteriological and physical-chemical quality. When a picture of the conservation potential of a region by sector, subsector, customer type and end use has been developed, it will provide a good understanding of the potential for potable water source substitution. Potable water use for some household chores could be substituted with rainwater, storm water and grey water, and the latter could be pre-treated to appropriate qualities at household level, if required. The needs of the end uses in the customer's premises may be matched with the quality of water, so that all water sources can be utilized to meet the water service needs (the concept of water quality cascading). The water quality cascading concept, which is commonly practised in industries, enables the water service providers to reduce not only the potable water demand, but also the effluent discharge into the sewer network, and ultimately, the environment.

To design WDM options, it is necessary to take advantage of opportunities that exist in the region effecting changes as a result of structural, operational, economic, awareness raising, public education, legal and institutional measures as discussed on page 27. In designing WDM options, it is important to identify options that are basic and will form the foundation of the programme. In IRP processes in Australia, the following options were examples of 'foundation' options considered for Australia IRP programmes:

- an ongoing education and public awareness programme;
- a customer advisory service to advise members of the public on how to participate in water efficiency programmes;

- permanent outdoor water use regulation that ensure sensible watering practices;
- universal customer metering;
- the use of regular billing cycles including customer feedback on bills;
- effective user-pays cost-reflective pricing; and
- basic system management, including systematic replacement of customer meters and calibration of bulk meters for more accurate water accounting.

In addition to the above listed foundation options, there is a large suite of water efficiency and potable water source substitution options that may make a significant impact is conserving water in the region at minimum programme costs. Table 3.4 show a broad spectrum of IRP options considered for Australian Capital Territory (ACT).

Table 3.4. IRP options considered for the ACT study	
Demand Management Options	Other Options
Pricing & information/awareness	Source water substitution
AAA (i.e. use less than 9l/min) rated showerhead rebate	• Rainwater tank rebates -existing • Rainwater tank rebates - new development
Dual flush toilet programme	• Grey water rebates - existing
Residential indoor audit/tune up	• Grey water rebates - new developments • Residential growth - water sensitive urban
Washing machine rebate	design (smart growth)
Residential outdoor assessment (single residential)	• Non-residential smart growth
Public housing indoor audit/tune up	
Public housing outdoor assessment	Water efficiency measures for exported water
Residential development control plans (DCPs)	• Queanbeyan Water Conservation Credits (QWSC)
Certification at time of sale	Reuse Option
Minimum water efficiency performance standards	• Extension of North Canberra Effluent Reuse Scheme (NCERS)
General commercial/industrial & institutional audits/retrofits	
Targeted commercial/industrial audits/ retrofits	Supply Options • Enlarged Cotter Dam
Targeted institutional audits/retrofits	• Construction of a new dam at Naas River • Transfer of water from Tantangara Dam
Non-residential development control plans (DCPs)	
Active water loss management	

Source: Turner and White, 2003

After identifying the suite of options that are technically feasible, the next steps are to measure the estimated water savings and determine which WDM options have adequate 'economies of scale' to qualify for further evaluation. A first cut approximation of the savings could be obtained through theoretical consideration based on the flow-rate specifications of the devices/appliances, but these figures should be verified through parallel surveying of similar WDM programmes carried out in other regions. Water savings should take into account the life and/or the decay of the water appliances under consideration, as well as natural changeover from inefficient to efficient fixtures/fittings, so that the latter is not solely attributed to the WDM programmes.

The next step is to analyse the selected individual options and estimate full economic costs and benefits, where possible. IRP aims to compare a set of options and select those with the greatest net benefit to the economy and society as a whole. Hence, IRP depends on economic analysis, which cancels out foregone revenue of the service provider, with benefits to the customers. Financial analysis, which assesses who pays for each element of the options, may be carried out in parallel with the economic analysis, mainly for the purpose of allocating costs fairly between stakeholders and analysing the cash flow situation of individual stakeholders. The main stakeholders considered in the economic analysis are the water service provider, the government and the customers, but third parties may be responsible for other monetized and non-monetized costs/benefits, which need to be included in the analysis. The ideal situation is to include both costs and benefits (i.e. avoided costs), but owing to the complexity of the cost model for the benefits, many analyses are based on costs alone. All costs incurred by all stakeholders pertaining to a programme for the whole lifecycle must be included. Where possible, externalities that can be quantified should be included. A good example is the greenhouse gas emissions, which can now be traded on international or regional greenhouse trading schemes.

There are three main methods that can be used to compare the various options - the Internal Rate of Return (IRR), Annualized Costs (AC) and the Net Present Value (NPV). The IRP team in Australia recommends the use of NPV method, mainly because both IRR and AC methods are more suitable for financial analysis but have poor comparability properties for different commodities in the economy.

The NPV of a programme is the value of the stream of costs and benefits associated with the programme into the future, discounted back to the present, based on a predetermined discount rate, usually assumed to be the societal rate of discount (Hanley and Spash, 1993). NPV is a good method for comparing suites of options (overall response). On the other hand, the Average Incremental Costs (AIC) metric (or levelized cost) has been used for comparing individual options that make up the response. AIC is a preferred metric mainly because it is a 'constant price' of water for each option, is similar to the long run marginal costing for the supply, and takes into consideration the timing of the services provided.

The various options can then be compared using either the AIC price or the cost benefit ratio, depending on whether the benefits have been included in the computation. There are many ways of portraying the results in a graphical format. One useful way is to plot a 'supply curve' which ranks the various options according to the unit cost (on the y-axis) and the yield (on the x-axis) for each option. This curve could rank all options in the supply, potable water substitution and water conservation categories, or could focus on one or more of the categories. Figure 3.4 shows an example of a curve ranking the water conservation and potable water substitution options for ACT water resources management strategy, already discussed in Table 3.4 (above. Another useful way of depicting the results in a graphical format is to draw of graph showing how various programmes cumulatively contribute to the yield (i.e. demand reduction or supply in a specified year) compared to the business-as-usual reference case, over the project period. Figure 3.5 shows an example of such a curve, also based on the ACT case study.

With the various options ranked using a common cost metric and according to estimated potential water savings, an assessment of grouped options may be carried out to develop an optimum least cost response. This assessment will of necessity go beyond the scope of quantifiable parameters, and will therefore require a qualitative assessment of some factors. Hence, the need to have wide consultations with the representative stakeholder group and have deliberate citizen involvement in the process. With full participation of relevant stakeholders, the first step is to screen out those options that are not consistent with the strategic direction of the region, and those that are highly uncertain in terms of costs, potential yield or mode of implementation. The least cost response can then be developed by combining the remaining options, ranked according to lowest unit cost or highest benefit-cost ratio, and sequenced until the supply-demand gap is filled. Options sequencing ensures that the least cost options are implemented first.

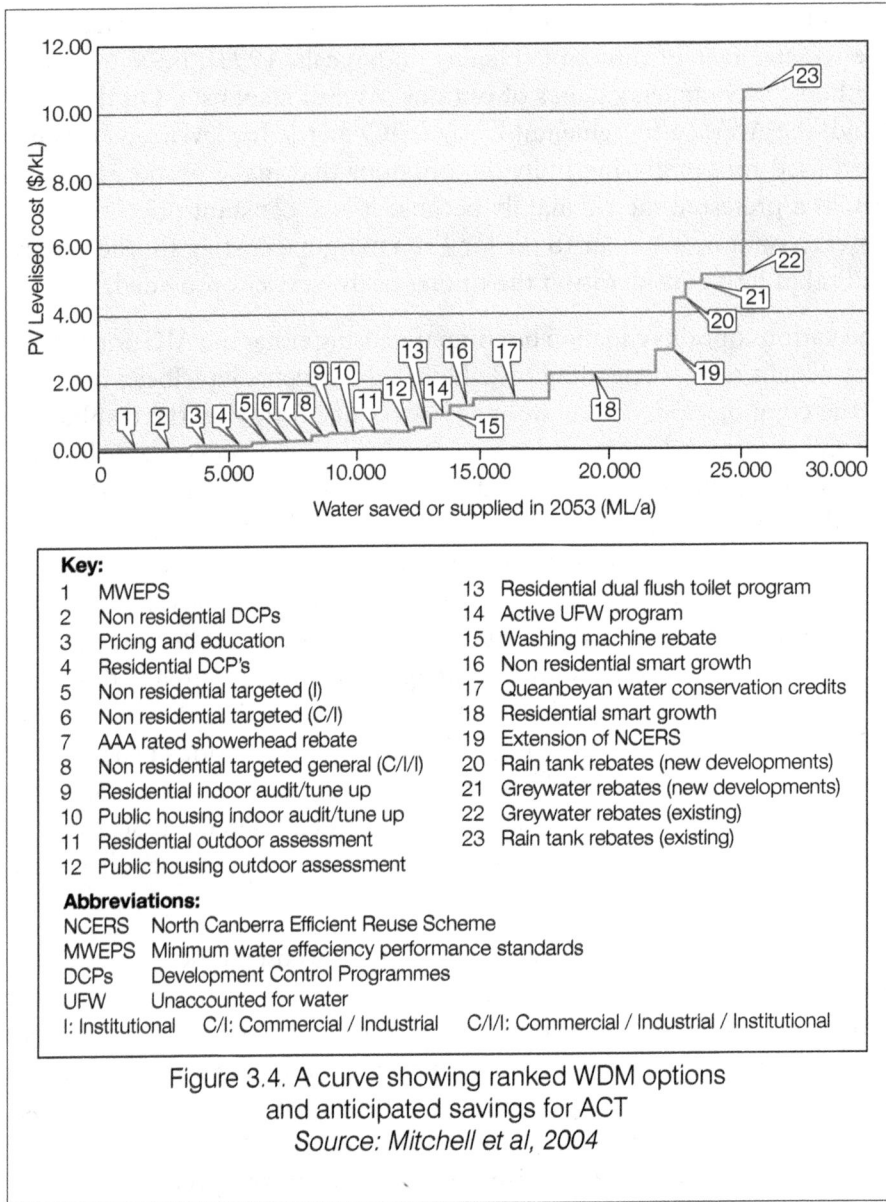

Figure 3.4. A curve showing ranked WDM options
and anticipated savings for ACT
Source: Mitchell et al, 2004

Key:

1	MWEPS	13	Residential dual flush toilet program
2	Non residential DCPs	14	Active UFW program
3	Pricing and education	15	Washing machine rebate
4	Residential DCP's	16	Non residential smart growth
5	Non residential targeted (I)	17	Queanbeyan water conservation credits
6	Non residential targeted (C/I)	18	Residential smart growth
7	AAA rated showerhead rebate	19	Extension of NCERS
8	Non residential targeted general (C/I/I)	20	Rain tank rebates (new developments)
9	Residential indoor audit/tune up	21	Greywater rebates (new developments)
10	Public housing indoor audit/tune up	22	Greywater rebates (existing)
11	Residential outdoor assessment	23	Rain tank rebates (existing)
12	Public housing outdoor assessment		

Abbreviations:

NCERS   North Canberra Efficient Reuse Scheme
MWEPS   Minimum water effeciency performance standards
DCPs   Development Control Programmes
UFW   Unaccounted for water
I: Institutional   C/I: Commercial / Industrial   C/I/I: Commercial / Industrial / Institutional

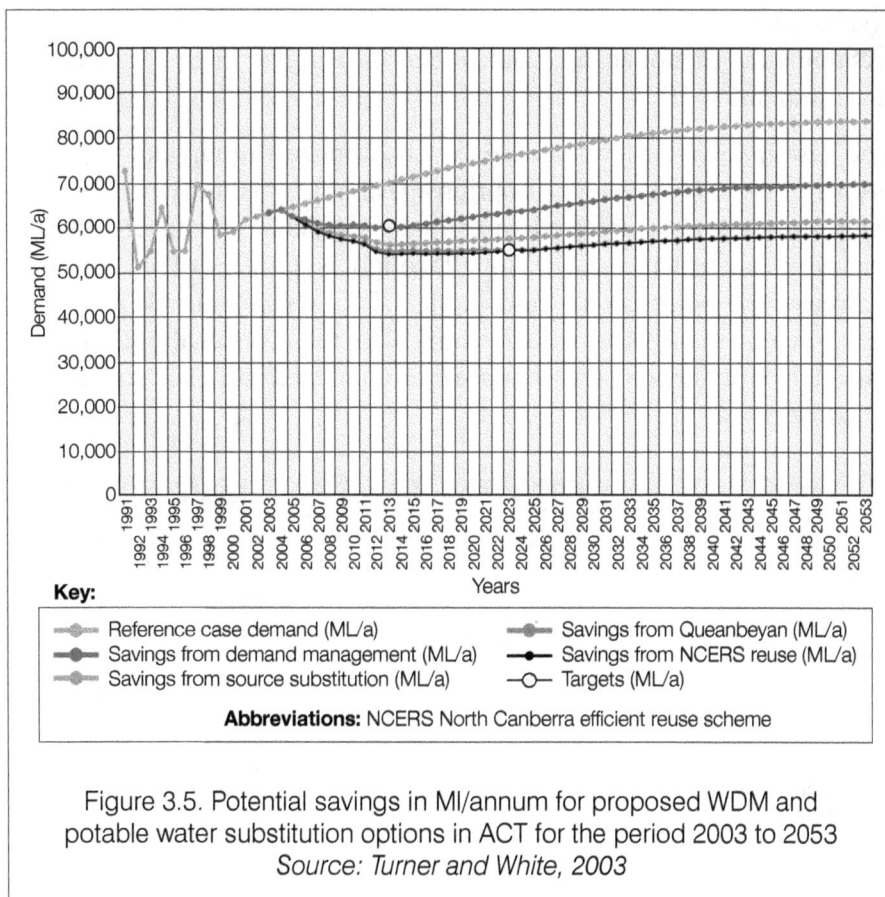

Figure 3.5. Potential savings in Ml/annum for proposed WDM and potable water substitution options in ACT for the period 2003 to 2053
Source: Turner and White, 2003

The qualitative assessment of the options should principally consider sustainability criteria, in which the steering team tests the performance of options under various scenarios, generates alternative responses and tests them. One of the guidelines commonly used for generating the sustainability criteria is what is known as the Triple Bottom Line (TBL) reporting, which was developed by Global Reporting Initiative (GRI), an official collaborating centre for the United Nations Environment Programme (UNEP). The TBL categories of criteria, which may be applied to the assessment of individual options or to the suite of options, are economic, environmental, and social aspects. Lundie et al (2005) suggested evaluating overall sustainability of water supply systems along the economic, human health, environmental, technical and social dimensions. On the other hand, the Water, Engineering and Development Centre (WEDC) employs the SHTEFIE acronym for assessing sustainability of water and sanitation systems, i.e. consideration of socio-cultural, health (public), technical/ technological, economic, financial, institutional and environmental aspects (Parr and Shaw, 1996).

The sustainability criteria should first be applied to individual options, prior to assessing the suites of options. Using the qualitative assessment, each option will be assessed to evaluate the level of impact for each criterion. Assessment may be done through assignment of an option to a three or five point Likert scale. Table 3.5 shows an example of criteria developed by the Australian IRP team. After the individual options have passed the sustainability test, they are then combined into a suite of options, into a response.

Table 3.5. Criteria developed for assessment of supply and demand-side options		
Environmental	Social	Risk/Feasibility
Terrestrial impact	Equity between socio-economic groups	Technical
Water quality and river health	Inter-catchment equity	Public acceptance
Ecosystems values	Landscape, amenity and recreational values	Risk of non-delivery of the option
Resource use efficiency	Health	Health and safety risks
Environmental sinks - air, land and river	Inter-generational equity	System reliability
		Institutional

The next step is to apply the sustainability criteria to the suite of options (i.e. response level), assessing characteristics such as:

- robustness with respect to potential challenges, e.g. climate change, population growth rates, required skills, supply-side delays;
- the range of diversity of options and customers targeted;
- contingency or overlap between annual available yield and projected demand; and
- flexibility and potential for adaptive management.

These response-level criteria can be used to develop alternative responses, which could then be assessed through scenario analysis. Scenario analysis is a tool used to understand and manage uncertainties, which are normally associated with projecting water demand and planning for water supply. Scenario analysis tests key assumptions that have been adopted for the

IRP process, by assessing the impact on alternative responses when the assumptions in place have been varied. Examples of assumptions that might be considered for scenario analysis are:

- low and high population projections;
- high and low per capita demand projections;
- significant risk of long term climate change impacting rainfall and evaporation;
- variation or introduction of environmental flow requirements;
- unexpected economic growth or decline in particular sectors;
- pessimistic up-take rates for demand management options and lower than expected conservation outcomes from demand-side measures; and
- pessimistic timetables for delivery of supply-side options.

To come up with an optimal response, it will be necessary to bring together the results of application of the sustainability criteria and scenario analysis so as to compare the various alternative responses that have been generated in the previous steps. In carrying out the comparisons, the 'least cost' response should be maintained as the basic reference case, as it is a core principle of the IRP process. The complexity of the optimizing process will depend on the scope of the problem and the context, and could be straightforward or may require significant analysis and iterations, more easily done through modelling. When the decision-making process gets more complex, decision support tools such as multi-criteria analysis (MCA) decision aids could be used to assist stakeholders make good decisions. MCA tools can be used to filter options and to test the impact of filtering on the overall cost of the suite of options, thereby supporting the stakeholders in the decision making process.

Implementation of the selected response

Implementation of the IRP response is a big programme and requires sound planning. The first activity in the planning for implementation is to form a stakeholder reference group, which will most likely involve a broader group than those who participated in the IRP steering committee, so as to obtain wider input into the implementation process. Specifically, all agencies that are likely to pay or contribute funds for various components of the proposed response should be members of the stakeholder reference group. Others are those agencies that will be directly involved in the implementation process, as well as representatives of those that will be affected by the programme. Early engagement of multiple stakeholders will ensure that an enabling environment is created at national, regional and local levels, support is gained from the relevant implementing organizations, and individuals with the appropriate skills and authority in various organizations buy into the implementation process.

From the wider stakeholder reference group, a WDM team should be formed, comprising individuals with the necessary skills and experience, to oversee the effective implementation of the programme. The team will require a diversity of skills such as project management, public relations and communication management, education and training, administration, finance and record keeping, economics, data collection and analysis, and contract management. Only a few members of the core team may need to be engaged on this programme on a full-time basis, the number depending on the complexity of the programme. Some of WDM team may work on the WDM programme only on a part-time basis as they continue with their normal posting, in which case it is recommended that the full time equivalent (FTE) of the team be catered for in the programme costs. Continuous training and capacity development programmes for the WDM team should mitigate against the effects of staff attrition.

One of the first roles of the WDM team is to verify the costs drawn during the planning process and develop budget plans for the programme that will cover management, administration, marketing, capital costs, and ongoing costs. The budget estimates should cover short and long-term periods and also indicate who pays for what and over what period. The budget estimates will have to be refined continuously, in line with real prices and real participation rates. In the short term, the cash flow position of the water service provider may be negative, which may require subsidies from the central government, or an increase in water service tariffs, in order to ensure revenue neutrality. Other key roles for preparation of the programme implementation include:

- development of a communication strategy that will ensure that the objectives and scope of the programme are well disseminated to key stakeholders and all sections of society;
- preparation of tender documents for contracting out components of the response, if this is applicable;
- identification of the training needs, before and during implementation of the programme for the WDM team, external collaborators, and individual customer groups;

- identification of data gaps, based on the sensitivity analysis carried out earlier (i.e. application of the sustainability criteria and scenario analysis), with a view of filling these gaps at the pilot stage;
- development of a schedule for monitoring and evaluation to include the evaluation needs, methods, timing, and types of data to be collected and how they will be analysed and stored;
- development of a mechanism for coordinating with other organizations involved in the programme, or doing a similar programme; and
- development of an implementation plan, a document that describing who, what, where, when and how the preferred response will be implemented, monitored and evaluated.

To test out the various components of the programme, it is recommended that a pilot programme should be undertaken before full-scale implementation. Piloting the programme will enable the WDM team to test specific aspects of the programme implementation such as project management, contractual arrangements, uptake rate, effectiveness of the communication strategy, methods and logistics of programme delivery, and effectiveness of the training programmes. Piloting is also a very useful and low-cost method of collecting data/information that was missing at the planning stage. It will also provide a basis for carrying out a preliminary evaluation of whether the desired outcomes are being achieved. Based on the findings of the pilot phase, improvements can then be made to the implementation plan, before implementing the full programme.

Monitoring, evaluating and reviewing the response

Monitoring and evaluation (M&E) of outcomes and processes of the individual WDM programmes, which should be embedded in the implementation plan, need to start at the piloting stage, and continue during full implementation. The implementation plan should specify, with respect to M&E, what data and information will need to be collected, how it will be collected/stored, how and when it will analysed, and how the M&E information will be used. M&E should investigate outcomes of participation rates, water savings and total/unit costs. Programmes with a strong focus on education and behaviour change may also evaluate changes in community knowledge, attitudes and behaviour, with the use of qualitative methods such as in-depth interviews and focus group discussions. M&E of implementation processes should investigate customer/stakeholder satisfaction and lessons learnt by the implementation team.

In the residential sector, participation rates may easily be obtained by carrying out a survey (by telephone, post, door-to-door etc) of a random sample of participants in the WDM programme, to find out whether they have actually implemented the WDM option(s). If the respondents have not implemented the option(s), they should be asked to state what the barriers are, and what might be done to overcome them. The participation rates for the non-residential sector should be easier to obtain, given smaller target numbers. Water savings in the residential sector may be measured using customer meter data, using participant and control/comparison methods (including matched pairs comparison), or through regression analysis. In the non-residential sector, measuring water savings attributable to the WDM programme may entail accurate sub-metering, and/or measuring water use as a function of the production process.

It is important to monitor and evaluate the costs of the WDM programme so as to establish the actual unit cost (financial) borne by the water service provider. M&E should also capture the costs (both capital and operating expenditure) borne by other stakeholders, so that the actual overall (economic) unit cost of the programme is obtained. In the non-residential sector, it may also be useful to establish the payback periods of the WDM measures, and energy savings there from, so that the information can be used to aid the promotion/sensitization strategy.

Measuring customer/stakeholder satisfaction is an important process-based M&E activity, which may be accomplished through customer satisfaction surveys or interviews. The results of the inquiry can then be used to improve the way the programme is designed and implemented. This form of research can be extended to also investigate what are the motivations and barriers to the uptake of WDM measures. It is also important to obtain the perspectives of stakeholders who are not customers, such as plumbers and housing estate contractors, which may contribute to improving the effectiveness of the WDM programmes. Another key aspect for M&E is the level of partnership between the project managers, customers and other relevant stakeholders.

After monitoring and evaluating individual programmes, the next step is to assess the full suite of programmes, focusing on the comparative advantages and disadvantage of programmes relative to each other, and how the programmes contribute to achieving the overall objective of reducing the supply-demand gap. Documentation of the evaluation carried out could then be presented to the stakeholder reference group to consider whether some programmes should be removed. Lessons learnt through the M&E

process should be captured, and documented so that institutional memory and organizational learning is maximized. This information will also be very useful for the overall IRP review process.

Conducting a thorough review process is an important step for initiating a new beginning for a subsequent cycle of the IRP process. It is a springboard for adaptive management, and aims at analysing the whole IRP process from a few different angles. All the relevant documentation made during the IRP process should be collated to enable the review process to take place. A recommended framework is to adopt the Soft Systems Methodology (SSM) (Checkland, 1999) and examine three key aspects of performance of the IRP process:

- efficiency - whether the conversion of inputs into outputs was achieved with as few resources as possible, and how the benefits compare with the costs;
- effectiveness - whether the desired objectives set originally have been achieved; and
- efficacy - what was the apparent worth or value of the intervention, in terms of user satisfaction, participatory inclusiveness and social equity?

Part of the review process is to reflect on what worked and what did not work for each step of the IRP process. Consultations/interviews should be held with the people involved in the IRP process at the decision-making level, as well those involved in conducting various parts of the analysis, modelling, implementation and evaluation. After collating, analysing and synthesizing the various secondary and primary data, a review report should be compiled, taking into consideration the target audience. The results should be disseminated using various pathways, including through a stakeholders' workshop.

IRP for cities of developing countries

Why apply IRP in cities of developing countries?

The previous section documents the IRP process as applied in Australia. Similar frameworks have been used by water service providers in other industrialized countries, particularly the United States, to apply the IRP for their strategic planning. Often, various IRP components are also separately applied for strategic planning by water service providers in cities of developing countries. However, there is no evidence so far in the international literature showing a wholesale application of IRP in cities of developing countries. The drivers for water service providers to apply IRP will vary from one context to another. For instance, a major driver for utilities in Australia has been the persistent drought conditions in these regions. The situation may be different in many developing countries, where there is no comparable deficiency of water resources in the service provider's catchment area. Water service providers in developing countries may need to carry out IRP as an avenue for incorporating demand management (WDM) approaches, for various other reasons.

WDM approaches are important to utilities in low-income countries for several reasons. Urban water service providers have not coped with demands from the escalating urban populations, mainly due to inadequate capacity in terms of capital finances, human resources and institutional framework. Low-income settlements of many cities in developing countries receive poor or no service from the utility mainly due to low density of the distribution pipelines, low production capacities at the treatment plants, and/or a combination of both. Because of the latter, many water distribution networks are operated in an intermittent water supply mode. Another contributing factor for intermittent water supply is the high levels of non-revenue water in many distribution networks, sometimes ranging over 50%. IRP could be applied to the different situations to establish whether WDM tools could be applied both on the sides of the service provider and the customers to turn the situation around or even make a viable difference in enhancing the service levels.

Connected with the point mentioned above, if water service providers in low-income countries have to operate the water distribution network intermittently, the question of equitable distribution usually comes into play. Experience has shown that usually the rich and most powerful in society obtain higher levels of service than households that are socially and economically disadvantaged. The advantages for the richer members of society stem from three main factors:

- they normally live in the best town locations which are well networked with probably better hydraulic properties;
- if they live in geographical locations which cannot induce good hydraulic properties during flow regimes, they usually have the capacity to invest in coping strategies; and
- they have a higher influence in the decision-making process for water service provision.

How can IRP be adapted for cities of developing countries?

IRP is a new concept, even for some water service providers in industrialized countries. Its application requires not only a multi-skilled planning team, but also high quality data. The need to convince the political leadership about the usefulness of IRP is higher in developing countries, where institutions are less functional and resources are scarcer. Furthermore, it will be more challenging to bring together the key relevant stakeholders, as sectors in developing countries tend to work in a more fragmented manner, sometimes using different development frameworks imposed upon them by various international funding agencies. Other specific aspects of IRP that need to be adapted for cities of developing countries are shown in Table 3.6.

Table 3.6. Key elements of the IRP for adaptation for cities of developing countries	
Item	Issues calling for re-examination
Stakeholder participation	Need for mobilisation for participation. Municipal departments' participation is critical; Widen the scope to include users' associations, academia, government, the private & NGO sectors; Training/capacity development of key stakeholders is more critical in developing countries.
Data collection	Start with available data; aim at incremental improvements in quality and quantity of data.
Demand forecasting	Start with sector aggregation; carry out case studies in different market segments; cater for various levels on the sanitation ladder such as pour flush pit latrines and low-cost sewerage; cater for town expansion.
Options analysis	Emphasis on water loss management in distribution systems; Emphasis on leakage management on the side of the customer, especially in public properties; Metering of customer properties; minimizing errors in measurement and illegal connections are key foundation options for WDM; Cater for improved service levels in line with improving living standards and hygiene & public health education; consider affordability and willingness to pay at household & national levels.
Implementation	Seek political buy-in by emphasizing monetary benefits; start with a pilot project & scale up. Promote WDM measures by water services as a way of reducing operational costs, especially energy costs Promote WDM measures by customers as a way of reducing water bills.

Source: adapted from Kayaga & Smout, 2008

Water professionals in low-income countries could, through global partnerships such as the International Water Association (IWA) specialist groups, learn from the experience of their counterparts elsewhere to adapt such new and useful concepts, and apply them through suitable local actions to their operating environment.

Strategic planning for WDM in Alexandria

A learning alliance of key stakeholders in Alexandria worked together with external research facilitators from the SWITCH project to develop a Strategic Plan for Integrated Urban Water Management. An important part of the process was the preparation of strategy studies on particular topics to be synthesised in the Strategic Plan: ground water potential; water demand management urban water system modelling; desalination; governance; storm water management; waste water management; social inclusion; and financial sustainability. A common Vision was agreed for 2037 and three possible scenarios for development and population growth, as shown in Box 3.3. Adopting an IRP perspective, it was agreed that options for water supply (including source substitution using groundwater, wastewater or desalinated water as well as water conservation measures) would all be analysed in terms of cost per m^3 of water supplied or saved.

The demand management study identified 10 possible strategies for water demand management in Alexandria:

1. Minimize physical and commercial losses from pipe networks.
2. Regular detailed monitoring of production, transfers to other areas, demands and losses.
3. Maximize water use efficiency in commercial premises and offices
4. Maximize industrial water use efficiency
5. Maximize household water use efficiency
6. Use alternative sources for some water uses
7. Capacity building of water company in WDM and partnerships with other organizations to reduce physical and commercial losses and increase end-use efficiency
8. Continue coordination between Alexandria water company and the Ministry of Water Resources and Irrigation
9. Increasing the tariff gradually , taking into account the different categories of users
10. Expand awareness and enforcement of laws

Box 3.3. Vision for urban water management in Alexandria in 2037 and possible scenarios

In 2037, we envision a proud water city where available water resources are managed in an integrated manner, with the participation of all citizens, and are used effectively for development within a framework of environmental sustainability, where all citizens have access to high quality (meeting national norms), reliable, sustainable, and affordable water and sanitation services and benefit from a clean and healthy environment. This includes:

- A clean and well managed aquatic environment (coastal zones and water bodies e.g. Lake Maryout)
- Provided by a renewed and upgraded network
- With full separation of sanitation and (agricultural and rainwater) drainage networks
- With treatment and reuse of agricultural, industrial, and domestic wastewater
- With agricultural water use managed as part of a city wide water management plan

Worst case scenario
In 2037, Alexandria is a city characterized by:
- Continued explosive population growth (summer population 12 million)
- A weak and stagnant economy
- Low availability of Nile water which is 40% less than in 2007 (due to increased national water demand and/or climate change)
- Increased risk of flooding (due to sea level rise)
- Poor availability of financial resources.

Best case scenario
In 2037, Alexandria is a city which:
- Has a population which has largely stabilized (at 8 million)
- Is benefiting from a dynamic and fast growing economy
- Has a guaranteed allocation of Nile water similar to that of 2007
- Has a positive scenario related to climate change (with sea level rise minimum and increased rainfall)
- Benefits from the new vitality of the Egyptian economy which means that financial resources are readily available.

Business as usual
In 2037, Alexandria continues to be a city dealing with considerable uncertainty:
- Population is 10 million, and continues to grow.
- National allocation of Nile water is 20% less than in 2007
- Economic growth has been steady but unspectacular
- Rising sea levels are starting to threaten some parts of the city.

Source: SWITCH (2011)

These options were analysed in terms of the potential quantities of water that could be saved, and how the strategy could be taken forward. The WDM study was complemented by the other studies, including the urban water system modelling which quantified various source substitution options: grey water re-use, roof water use and road water reuse. The SWITCH Project also undertook a Water Demand Management Demonstration in Alexandria, focusing on the following:

- Non-Revenue Water: Setting up a District Meter Area; Leak detection; Pipe repair; Commercial loss analysis
- Meters & Connections: Household survey & Meter installation
- Water Efficiency: Planning Tool; Efficiency device availability and water saving potential
- Alternative water sources: landscape irrigation

Work on the planning tool included analysis of nine demand management options and seven supply options, according to how much water they could save or supply in 2037, and the unit cost of the water (calculated in US dollars as the present value of the costs and the volume of water, using a discount rate of 7%). These options are listed in Table 3.7.

It was estimated that more than 300 million m³ could be saved per year by demand management measures costing less than €0.10 per m³, which is a quarter of the price of the cheapest supply option. These results are illustrated in the supply curve shown in Figure 3.7, assuming that the least cost options are implemented first. A saving of 300 million m³ per year represents about 30% of the current water supply and would make a major contribution to meeting the increased demand for water services in Alexandria in 2037. Using water more efficiently in this way would also reduce the energy consumption by the water industry, and the emission of greenhouse gases.

The Alexandria case study shows that demand management measures have considerable potential in the cities of developing countries. It also demonstrates how local studies can be used to analyse options and identify priority options for further investigation and implementation.

Table 3.7. Demand and supply options modelled for Alexandria			
Code		Water saved or supplied in 2037 (Mm³/year)	Unit cost (PV$/PVm³)
DM1	Household water saving fittings retrofit	26	0.08
DM2	Toilet replacement program for households	6	0.53
DM3	Tourist & commercial buildings audit and retrofit	30	0.11
DM4	Government buildings audit and retrofit	41	0.08
DM5	Industrial facilities audit and retrofit	34	0.06
DM6	System leakage reduction	59	0.02
DM7	Tariff reform	57	0.00
DM8	Agricultural efficiency offsets (to increase supply to the city)	75	0.01
DM9	Appliance efficiency regulation (at the national level)	21	0.02
S1	Desalination for coastal resorts	42	1.15
S2	Wastewater reuse for industrial properties	32	0.60
S3	Agricultural drainage water desalination and reuse for industries and coastal resorts (non-potable use)	62	0.63
S4	Wastewater reuse for agriculture	63	0.48
S5	Groundwater for urban green space irrigation	18	0.48
S6	Local wastewater reuse for new developments (incorporating decentralised sewer systems)	37	0.40
S7	Local wastewater reuse and nutrient recovery (incorporating decentralised sewer systems and urine diversion)	37	0.58

Source: Retamal and White 2011, White et al. 2011

57

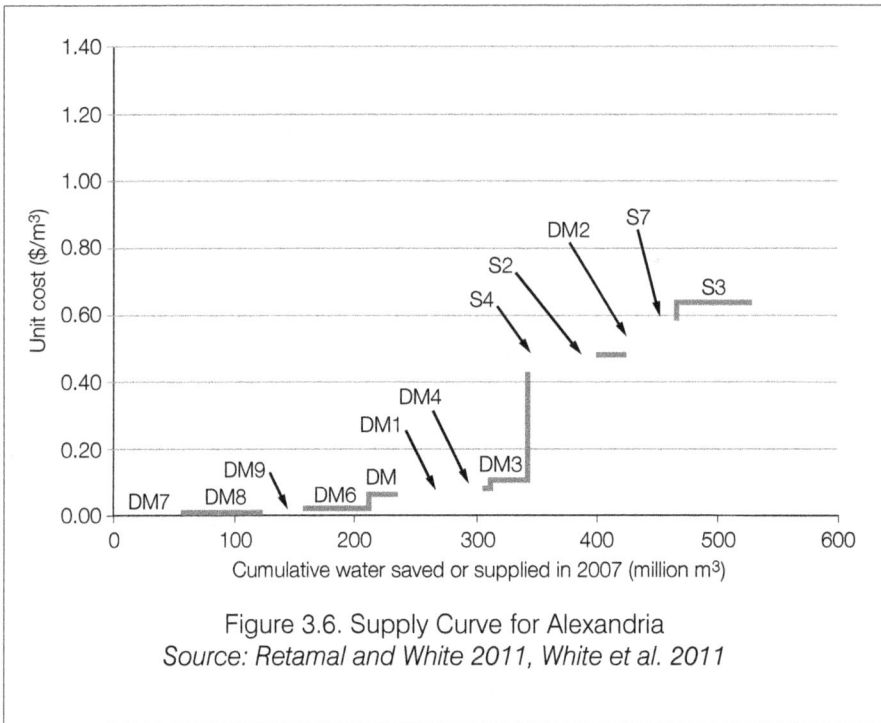

Figure 3.6. Supply Curve for Alexandria
Source: Retamal and White 2011, White et al. 2011

References

Beecher, J.A. (1995) Integrated resource planning fundamentals, *Journal AWWA*, 87(6), 34-48.

Botica, R. and White, S. (1996) Kalgoorlie-Boulder: The Water Efficient City, *Water: Journal of the Australian Water and Wastewater Association*, 23(5), 14-17.

Checkland, P (1999) *System thinking, system practice*, John Wiley and Sons Ltd, Chichester, UK.

Cordell, D.J.; Robinson, J.E. and Loh, M.T.Y. (2003) Collecting residential end use data from primary sources: Dos and Don'ts, in: *IWA Efficient 2003: Efficient Use and Management of Water for Urban Supply Conference, 2-4 April 2003, Tenerife, Spain.*

Grigg, N. S. (1998) A new paradigm for water management, in: *International Symposium on water resources management, 5-8 October, 1998, Gramado, Brazil.*

Hanley, N.D. and Spash, C. L. (1993) *Cost-Benefit Analysis and the Environment*, Edward Elgar Press, London, UK.

Howe, C. and White, S. (1999) Integrated resource planning for water and wastewater – Sydney case studies, *Water International*, 24(4), 356-362.

Kayaga, S. and Smout, I. (2008) Integrated Resource Planning: a vital tool for utilities in low-income countries, in: *Proceedings of the 33rd WEDC International Conference, Accra, Ghana, April 2008.* WEDC, Loughborough University, UK.

Lundie,S.; Ashbolt, N.; Livingston,D.; Lai, E.; Kärrman, E.; Blaikie, J. and Anderson, J. (2005) *Methodology for Evaluating the Overall Sustainability of Urban Water Systems,* Centre for Water and Waste Technology, University of New South Wales, Australia.

Mackay, R., and Last, E. (2010) SWITCH city water balance: a scoping model for integrated urban water management. *Reviews in Environmental Science and Biotechnology.* 9:291–296

Maddaus, W.O. and Maddaus, L.A. (2001) Water Demand Management Within the Integrated Resource Planning Process, Paper presented at: *Efficient 21 Conference, 21-23 May 2001, Madrid, Spain.*

Mitchell, C.; Turner, A. Cordell, D.; Fane, S. and White, S. (2004) Water conservation is dead: Long live water conservation, in: *2nd IWA Leading Edge Conference on Sustainability in Water Limited Environments, Sydney, Australia.*

Parr, J. and Shaw, R. (1996) Technical Brief No. 49: Choosing an Appropriate technology, *Waterlines* 15(1), 15-18.

Retamal, M. and White, S. (2011) *Integrated supply-demand planning for Alexandria, Egypt: water efficiency study and business case analysis for water demand management.* Prepared for CEDARE/SWITCH by the Institute for Sustainable Futures, Sydney.

Sharifi, M.A. (2003) Integrated planning and decision support systems for sustainable water resources management: concepts, potentials and limitations, Resource paper presented at: *Seminar on Water Resource Management for Sustainable Agricultural Productivity, 6-11 October 2003, Lahore, Pakistan.*

Swisher, J.N.; Jannuzzi, G. and Redlinger, R.Y. (1997) *Tools and Methods for Integrated Resource Planning: improving energy efficiency and protecting the environment,* (Working Paper No. 7), UNEP Collaborating Centre on Energy and Environment, Denmark.

SWITCH (2010a) Sustainable Water management Improves Tomorrow's Cities' Health (SWITCH) Project Description of Works, Months 49-60.

SWITCH (2010b) "Strategic Planning for Integrated Urban Water Management", SWITCH Policy Briefing Note 2, available from http://www.switchurbanwater.eu/outputs/index.php

SWITCH (2011) "Alexandria Integrated Urban Water Management Plan for year 2037: A Vision for the Water Future of Alexandria".

Tellus Institute (2000) *Best Practices Guide: Integrated Resource Planning for Electricity*, The Electricity Group, Institute of International Education, Washington DC.

Turner, A. and White, S. (2003) *ACT Water Strategy: Preliminary Demand Management and Least Cost Planning Assessment - Final Report*, Institute for Sustainable Futures, University of Technology, Sydney, Australia.

Turner, A.; White, S. and Bickford, G. (2005) The Canberra Least Cost Planning Case Study, in: *IWA International Conference on the Efficient Use and Management of Urban Water, Santiago, Chile, 15-17 March 2005*.

Turner, A.; Willets, J.; Fane, S.; Guirco, D.; Kazaglis, A. and White, S. (2006) *Planning our future urban water resources: A guide to demand management in the context of integrated resource planning*, Institute of Sustainable Futures, University of Technology, Sydney.

White S. (1999) Integrated Resource Planning in the Australian water industry, in: Proceedings of the CONSERV99, *American Water Works Association, Monterey, California, USA, February 1999*.

White, S., Retamal, M., AbuZeid, K., Elrawady, M. And Turner, A. (2011) Integrated Resource Planning for Alexandria, Egypt. *6th IWA Specialist Conference on Efficient Use & Management of Water, Jordan 29 March – 2 April, 2011*

White, S., Robinson, J., Cordell, D., Jha, M. and Milne, G. (2003) *Urban water demand forecasting and demand management: Research needs review and recommendations*, Occasional Paper No. 9, Water Services Association of Australia (WSAA).

Part 2

Emerging Water Demand
Management Tools:
selected examples

4

Demand Management Options Model

Daniel van Rooijen, Sam Kayaga and Ian Smout

This paper has been submitted for presentation at the 35th WEDC International Conference in Loughborough, U.K

Need for water demand management

While the population in many industrialized countries is either decreasing or constant, the population in most developing countries is increasing rapidly, resulting in an overall global population increase. The current global population is estimated to be 6.9 billion people, of which 82% live in developing countries (UN-HABITAT, 2009). Consequently, per capita water availability is steadily declining. The water scarcity situation is compounded by the major impacts of climate change on the water resources, and the practical distribution problems concerned with time, space and affordability, leading to a widening gap between demand and supply in many parts of the world. The water scarcity situation will escalate in the urban areas of less developed regions where it is estimated that the urban population will increase from about 2.57 billion in 2010 to 3.95 billion in 2030, accounting for 94% of the global urban population growth in the period 2010-2030 (*ibid*).

The situation calls for mainstreaming Water Demand Management (WDM) in the strategic plans of cities. WDM may be defined as the development and implementation of strategies, policies and measures aimed at influencing demand, so as to achieve efficient and sustainable use of the scarce water resource (Savenije and van der Zaag, 2002). Another commonly used definition of WDM is '...adaptation and implementation of a strategy by a water institution to influence the water demand and usage in order to meet any of the following objectives: economic efficiency, social development, social equity, environmental protection, sustainability of water supply and services and political acceptability' (Jalil and Njiru, 2006, p.45). Most definitions of WDM allocate the initiative for WDM to the service provider, which is expected to develop policies and invest in measures to achieve efficient water use both within the water distribution network (i.e. management of non-revenue water) and at the end-users' premises. WDM contrasts with the conventional supply-driven approach to water resources management, whose response to the ever increasing water demand is development of new water sources.

There are five major categories of WDM measures (White and Fane, 2001): those measures that (i) increase system efficiency at the utility level; (ii) increase end use efficiency; (iii) promote locally available resources not currently being used, such as rainwater harvesting; (iv) promote substitution of resource use, e.g. use of waterless sanitation; and (v) use economic instruments to bring about an improvement in resource usage, such as use of tariffs. A service provider could implement and/or promote a combination of one or more options that exist under each category. Urban water managers and policy makers need to make correct choices of the most viable options that fit within the socio-cultural, political, economic and environmental context. Ideally, these choices take into consideration the vision of the key city stakeholders and identified scenarios over the longer-term period. This paper presents a decision support tool for urban water managers and planners, developed under the EU-funded SWITCH research project, for use in the 'city of the future'. The five-year SWITCH (Sustainable Water management Improves Tomorrow's City Health) project aimed at developing efficient and interactive urban water systems and services in the city's geographical and ecological setting, which are robust, flexible and responsive to a range of global change pressures.

The SWITCH research work on WDM adopted the Integrated Resource Planning (IRP) approach that embraces wider strategic planning principles and fits well with the integrated urban water resources management framework. First applied in the energy sector, IRP is an approach in which a full range of both supply-side and demand-side options are assessed against a common set of planning criteria. IRP is a systematic planning process that identifies the most efficient means of achieving the goals, while considering the costs of the project impacts on other societal objectives and environmental management goals. The main steps of carrying out an IRP process include (Turner et al, 2006): (i) analysis of the situation to identify factors influencing the supply-demand balance; (ii) forecasting future demand; (iii) setting planning objectives; (iv) considering a wide range of potential options, i.e. options analysis; and (v) planning to implement, undertaking a pilot programme and scaling up. The remainder of this paper focuses on the options analysis stage and describes a VENSIM model, a fairly simple decision support tool that uses a common cost metric to compare various options that may be adopted over a long-term planning horizon.

Introduction to the WDM Model in VENSIM

The WDM model was developed based on a scoping study carried out in Alexandria, Egypt, in which feasible options were identified through a participatory workshop attended by water managers, engineers and planners in the city. Figure 4.1 shows a mind map that was drawn to guide the development of the model. It shows WDM options feasible in a hypothetical city, our study setting. The Ventana Systems Environment (VENSIM) platform was chosen for developing the WDM model. VENSIM is a visual modelling tool that serves to conceptualize, document, simulate, analyse and optimize models of dynamic systems (VENSIM, 1998). The VENSIM tool has been used in a broad range of disciplines such as business, scientific, environmental, and social systems.

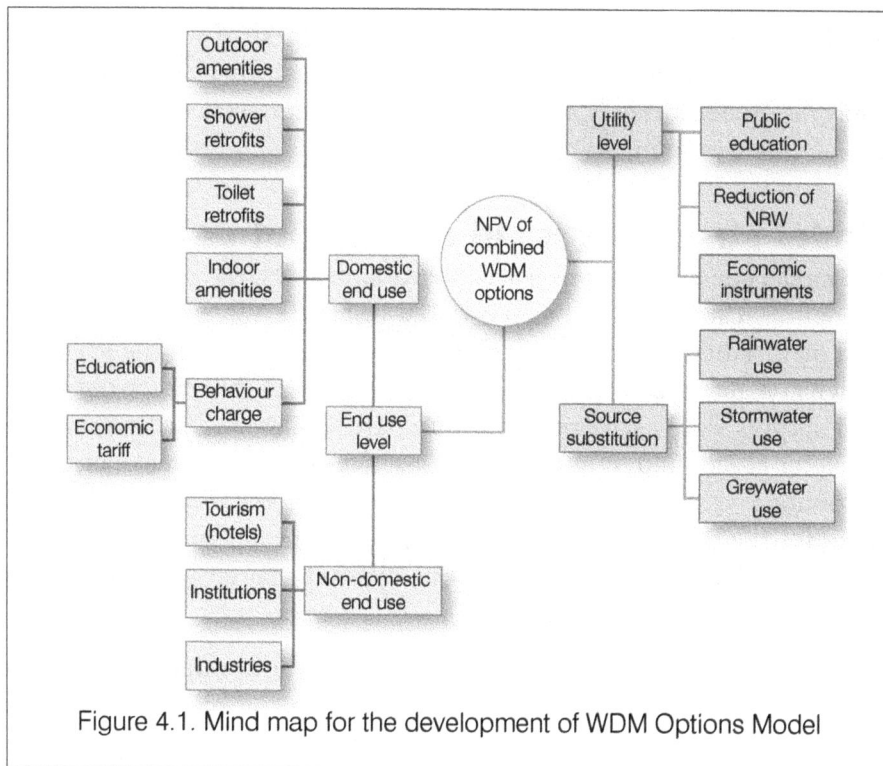

Figure 4.1. Mind map for the development of WDM Options Model

VENSIM fitted well with the requirement of the SWITCH research outputs, as it is simple, easy-to-use, interfaces with Excel input data, is user-built, and therefore is flexible. The model is constructed by entering and defining causal relationships between system variables. This information is used by the equation editor to define the relationships as formulae. The model can be changed, tested and analysed throughout the building process and the model allows its user to thoroughly explore the behaviour of the model. The VENSIM software has been used previously to develop an urban water balance modelling tool and was successfully applied in Hyderabad, India (van Rooijen et al., 2005). Other notable examples are modelling of water-energy systems (Medeazza & Moreau, 2006); simulation of soil erosion and nutrient impact (Ye, Wang & Yu, 2006) and evaluating the impact of inpatient payment strategy on hospital behaviour (Rauner and Schaffauser-Linzatti, 2002).

The WDM model was developed for a hypothetical city. The time frame of the model was set for a period of 30 years, say from 2010 to 2040. Some of the data used were obtained from the City of Alexandria, through a 'quick and rough' participatory scoping study. A significant amount of data input into the model is based on assumptions developed through a literature review of previous WDM measures in other countries such as the US, Europe and Australia. The cost-effectiveness of WDM options is very much dependent on local circumstances which vary for each city. To apply the model correctly, it is therefore important to collect the necessary sets of data pertaining to the city of interest.

Model structure, input and output data

The model consists of three levels, the variable level, the option level and the options category level, as illustrated in Figure 4.2. The number and type of variables may differ from one option to another. The variables shown in Figure 4.2 are with respect to the option of shower retrofits. The final outputs from each option however, are similar, and are expressions of 'water saved' and 'costs' of the respective option. The categories for the options were based on the four areas in which the measures could be taken for the hypothetical city. Similarly, it has been assumed that there are 12 feasible WDM options for this hypothetical city, categorized as shown in the mind map (Figure 4.1).

The model runs on a set of input data most of whose values are location specific. Other values are assumed constant. In the model, some data remain constant during the modelling period, while others always behave as variables. Model inputs consists of data for programme costs, water use (and savings) and response variables. In the absence of real data, assumptions were made, based on data and information from cities in a comparable context or calculated based on other data. These assumptions were informed by a combination of data in international literature, personal experience and expert opinion. The process of obtaining the variable data shown in Figure 4.2 above is described in more details in the following paragraphs.

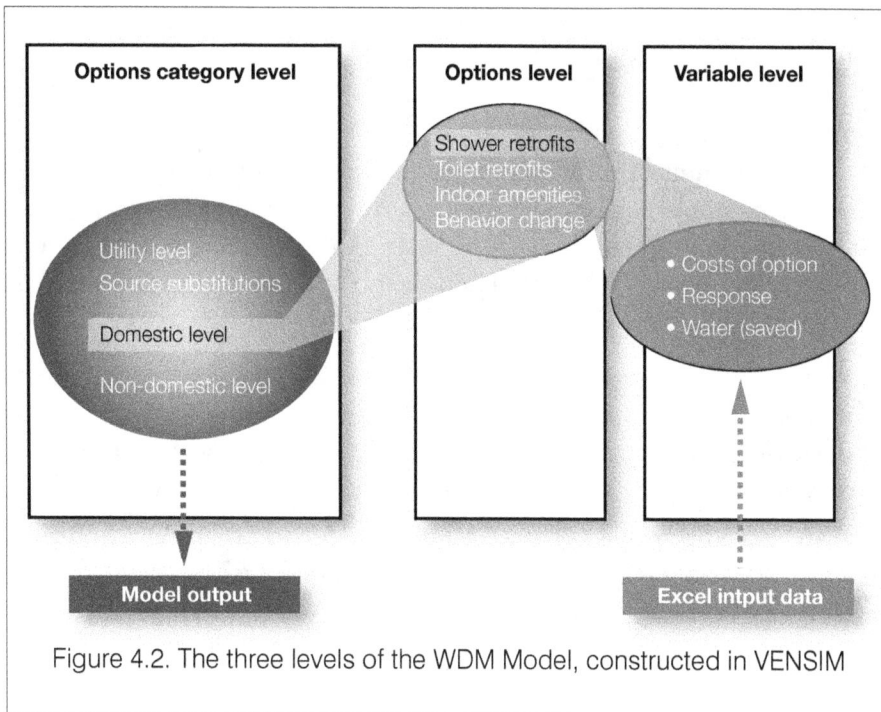

Figure 4.2. The three levels of the WDM Model, constructed in VENSIM

Costs of option

These are costs of the programme, incurred by the utility to implement or promote an option during the 30-year project period. Some options require high start-up costs with little or no follow up investment. Examples are retrofits of water saving devices such as toilet cisterns - with a long life time, which may not need further investments. On the other hand, some options, such as active leakage management of distribution networks require investments throughout the project period, probably at a decreasing scale. The Net Present Value (NPV) for each of the costs are computed for each year and summed up over the project period. The discount rate used for computing NPV is dependent on the social rate of return applicable to the study area. A figure of 7% was assumed for the hypothetical city. Cost figures used in this model were assumed based on parallel surveying with cities where WDM options studies have been carried out.

Response

The response variable represents the potential for uptake of the options. For options leading to water conservation at the end-use level, this is expressed as a fraction (%) of the target 'audience' for effecting change, such as households. In the case of storm water harvesting, the response variable is expressed as 'reuse factor', which shows the extent to which collected storm water may be used to save potable water.

Water saved

This is the amount of water saved per year as a result of a specific WDM option being implemented. These figures are estimated based on empirical data obtained through previous WDM studies conducted in various parts of the world, especially Australia and the USA. The input data depend on the option under consideration. Notable examples are described below:

- Water saved through use of efficient water devices. The volume saved will be directly proportional to the unit savings for each type of water device (e.g. showers, toilets, and taps) and response factor (i.e. the number of end users signing up) for the programme per year.

- Water saved through behavioural change due to an increase in tariffs. The water saved per household will depend on the average price elasticity of demand (Ed) in a given city. Water saved (Qd) will be determined by the function for Ed provided below, where P is the initial price, Qd is the initial demand, and P is the change in price. Ed is estimated through parallel surveying with comparable cities where tariff studies have been carried out (e.g. Arbues & Villanua, 2006):

$$E_d = \frac{\%\text{ change in quantity demanded}}{\%\text{ change in price}} = \frac{\Delta Q_d/Q_d}{\Delta P/P}$$

- Water savings through behavioural change due to public education. Empirical studies (e.g. Renwick and Green, 2000) have been conducted to estimate the effect of public education, and coefficients of water saved have been estimated. This information has been adapted for the hypothetical city, in order to estimate the potential water savings as a result of public education.

- Water saved through source substitution in the household such as rainwater harvesting and grey water reuse. Various studies (e.g. Dixon, Butler & Fewkes, 1999) have been carried out to estimate the potential for water source substitution at household level. Our assumed figures for potential average savings per household per year are based on empirical data from these case studies.

- Savings from storm water reuse. In a similar manner, empirical data from previous studies (e.g. Hatt, Deletic & Fletcher, 2006) have been used to estimate the fraction of storm water collected that could be reused per year in a city of a given surface area with specific physical characteristics, which receives a given average annual rainfall.

The input data are entered into an Excel spreadsheet. Colour coding is used to clarify the origin of the input data: those cells that require user-input are marked in light blue; cells that feed into the VENSIM model are marked in pink; and those marked in green are calculated by Excel and VENSIM. The model outputs for each of the WDM options are:

- Net Present Value of 'Water Saved' in m³, considered as a stream of benefits over the WDM project period;

- Net Present Value of 'Cost of Programme' in currency units (e.g. Euros for this hypothetical city), considered as a stream of costs over the WDM project period;

- the sum of 'Water Saved' in m³ during the project period;

- the sum of 'Cost of Programme' in currency units (e.g. Euros for this hypothetical city); and

- the Average Incremental Cost (AIC) or levelised cost: Net Present Value of 'Cost of Programme' divided by Net Present Value of 'Water Saved'

Other outputs of the model are the sums of 'Water Saved' and 'Cost of Programme' for all the WDM options for the whole project period. The VENSIM model outputs can be displayed in various forms of table and chart formats. Figure 4.3 shows an Excel sheet with data inputs and outputs.

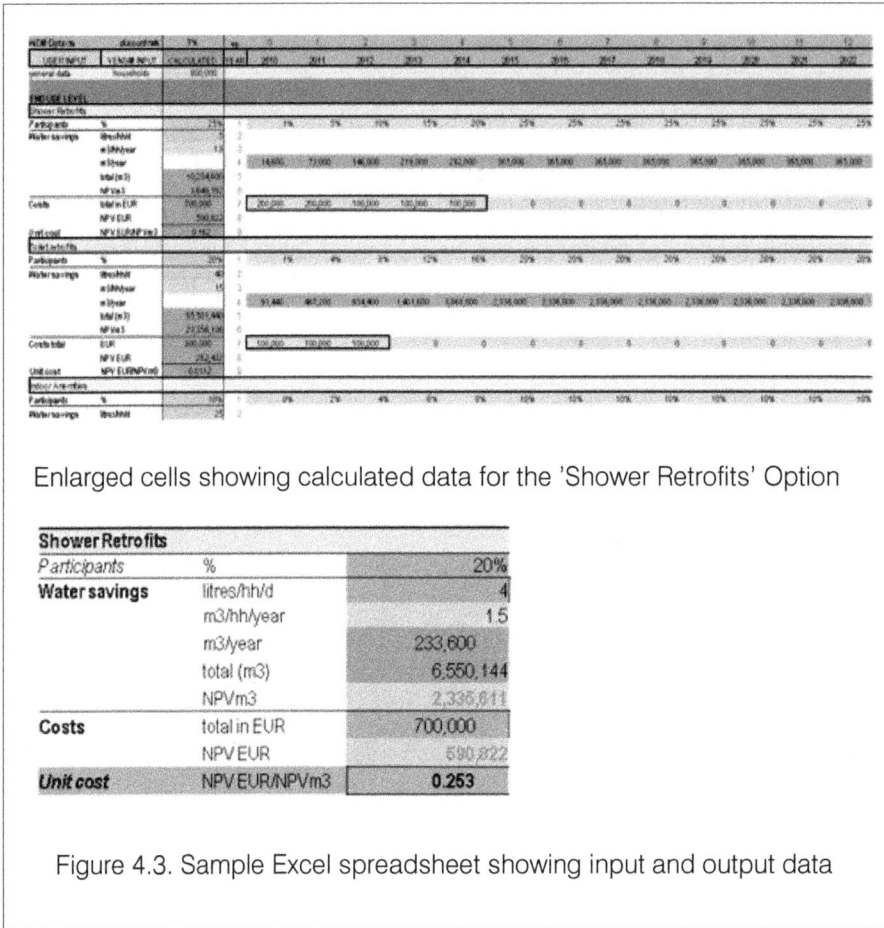

Enlarged cells showing calculated data for the 'Shower Retrofits' Option

Shower Retrofits		
Participants	%	20%
Water savings	litres/hh/d	4
	m3/hh/year	1.5
	m3/year	233,600
	total (m3)	6,550,144
	NPVm3	2,335,611
Costs	total in EUR	700,000
	NPV EUR	590,822
Unit cost	NPV EUR/NPVm3	0.253

Figure 4.3. Sample Excel spreadsheet showing input and output data

Comparison of WDM Options

The depth of analysis of options may vary depending on the planning goal as determined by the needs of the key stakeholders, the quality and scope of data input into the model, and the capacity of the team carrying out the analysis. Among the questions that could be answered by the WDM model are those indentified by Turner et al (2006) as:

- What suite of demand-reducing options can meet the WDM target?

- How much will these programmes cost the community as a whole and what level of investment in WDM is cost-effective in a specific region?

- What suite of options will best meet the long-term requirement for balancing supply and demand in this region at the lowest cost to the community?

Different cost perspectives may be applied for analysing WDM options. A financial analysis is usually undertaken to obtain the cost perspectives with respect to service providers, which provides an overview for cash flow analysis, so that appropriate arrangements may be put in place to meet their revenue needs. On the other hand, an economic analysis considers the net benefit to society as a whole, and includes the service providers' externality costs. The IRP approach strongly recommends application of economic analysis of WDM, since it seeks to determine which set of options have the greatest net benefit to the economy and society as a whole (*ibid*).

The Net Present Value (NPV) is the preferred method for comparing a suite of WDM options, mainly because it provides a monetary value that is comparable to currently known costs and benefits in the present. It is also a standard method used by national governments and international agencies to evaluate and compare programmes. Furthermore the use of Average Incremental Method (AIC) provides an equivalent 'constant price' comparison across scales, taking into consideration the timing of the service. As described above, the NPV of programme costs, potential water savings and AIC or levelized cost for each option are computed by the model. These values can also be displayed in graphical format, for ease of comparison. Figures 4.4 to 4.6 show examples of graphs plotted by the model from the hypothetical city data, through which comparison of the various WDM options can be displayed.

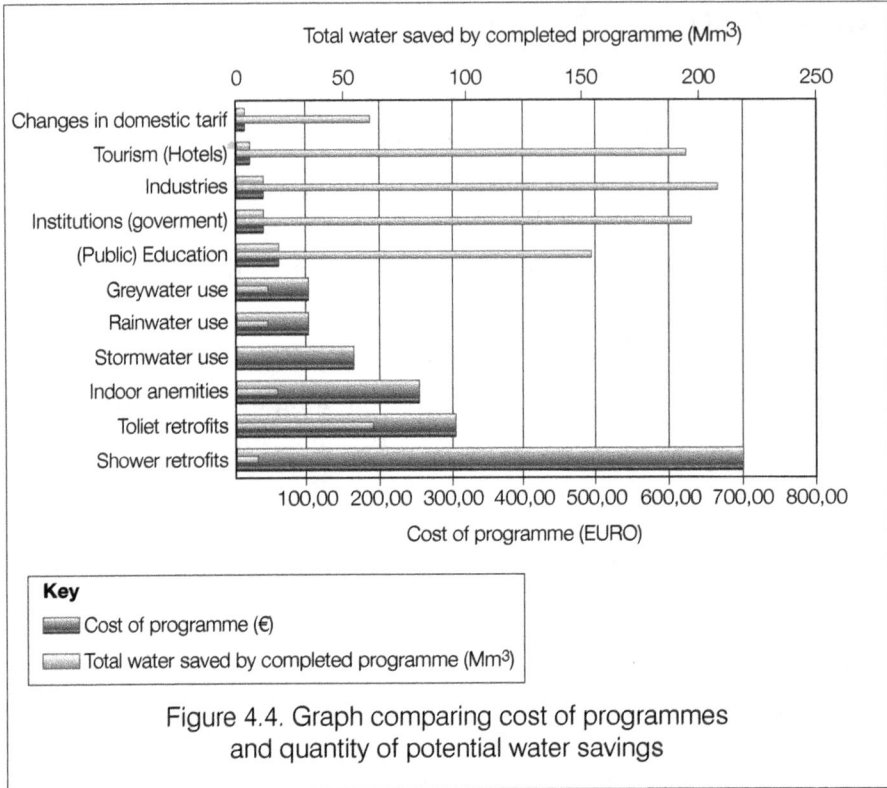

Figure 4.4. Graph comparing cost of programmes
and quantity of potential water savings

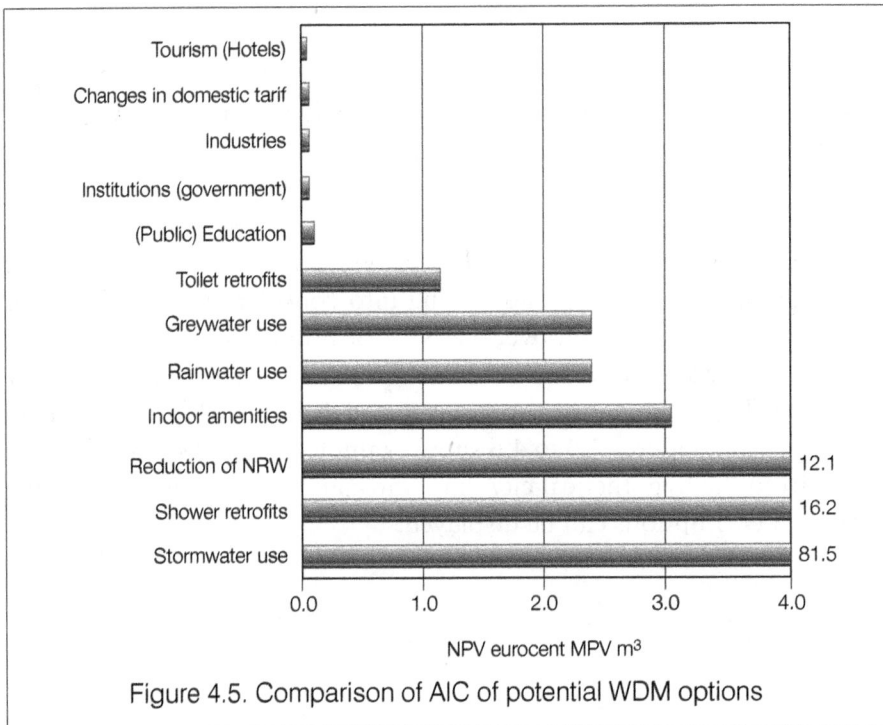

Figure 4.5. Comparison of AIC of potential WDM options

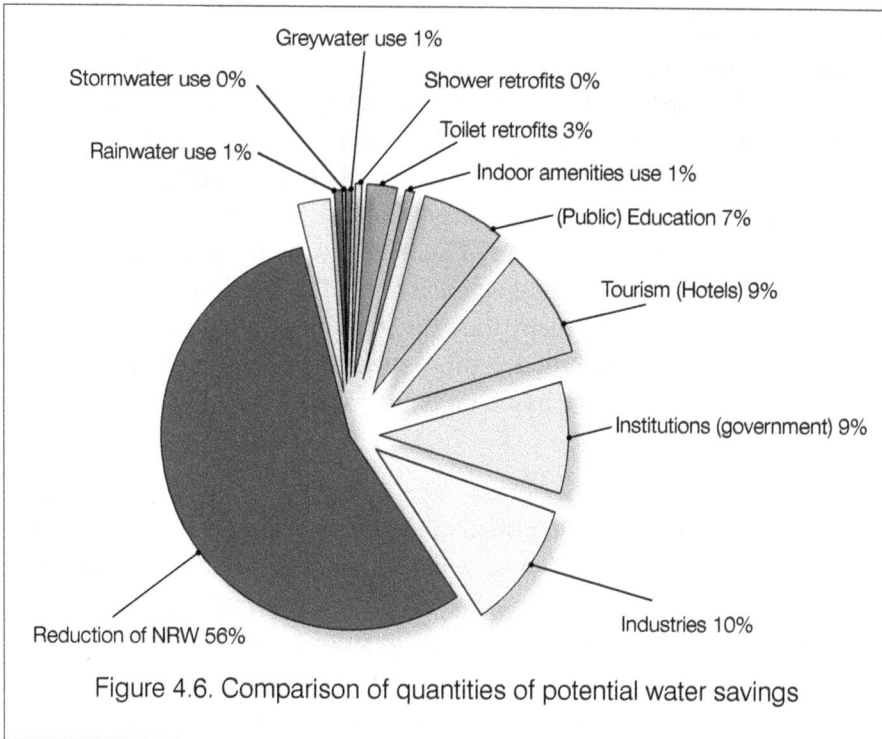

Figure 4.6. Comparison of quantities of potential water savings

In the figure: Greywater use 1%, Shower retrofits 0%, Stormwater use 0%, Toilet retrofits 3%, Rainwater use 1%, Indoor amenities use 1%, (Public) Education 7%, Tourism (Hotels) 9%, Institutions (government) 9%, Industries 10%, Reduction of NRW 56%

Limitations of the WDM Model

Similar to all other models, the quality of the output data is as good as the input data. This WDM model requires lots of data, some of which may be difficult to collect, particularly for urban water utilities in countries of the less developed regions, where management information systems may be underdeveloped. The model for the hypothetical city was developed using a series of assumptions based on review of international literature. This model has been developed only for illustration purposes, and its output data are deemed inaccurate.

This model was developed as a simple decision support tool that can be applied by urban water managers, engineers and planners with no skills of linear programming, and making use of whatever data are available. Although the VENSIM models are system-dynamic and are capable of simulating continuously-varying systems, they do not typically incorporate uncertainty about internal or external attributes of the systems, nor can they represent discrete events.

Conclusion

Often, decision support tools developed by research institutions are complex and sometimes inaccessible to practitioners. The WDM options model developed by WEDC as part of an output for the SWITCH Project is a simple decision support tool that can easily be applied by urban water engineers, planners and managers for ranking WDM options based on an economic cost benefit analysis. The WDM options model in VENSIM compares the costs and benefits of each option over a long term horizon, making it a good management tool for making strategic decisions. The model characteristics presented in this paper only give an example of what can be modelled, as they are based on data assumed for a hypothetical city.

Notes

This model utilizes a modelling shell made freely available by the VENSIM software owners at http://www.vensim.com/freedownload.html. The relevant files for running this model in its present illustrative format are available at the SWITCH website www.switchurbanwater.eu. To modify the model structure, one would require a professional version of the software, which can be purchased from Ventana Systems Inc. at a modest fee. The information on costs of VENSIM Professional is available http://www.vensim.com/buy.html. VENSIM Professional allows the user to add and modify the model settings, configurations, equations, etc. An extensive modelling guide is also available for free download at http://www.vensim.com/documentation.html.

Acknowledgements

This paper is based on research work that has been carried out as part of the Work Package 3.1 of the EU-funded SWITCH Project. We are grateful to the Institute for Sustainable Futures (ISF), University of Technology, Sydney, for their guidance and materials on the application of the Integrated Resource Planning (IRP) framework. We are also grateful to the stakeholders in Alexandria, who provided initial data that informed the scope of this model.

References

Arbués, F. and Villanúa, I., 2006, Potential for pricing policies in water resource management: estimation of urban residential water demand in Zaragoza, Spain, *Urban Studies*, 43(13): 2421-2442.

Dixon, A., Butler, D. and Fewkes, A. (1999) Water saving potential of domestic water reuse systems using grey water and rainwater in combination, *Water Science and Technology*, 39(5): 25-32.

Hatt, B.E, Deletic, A. and Fletcher, T.D. (2006) Integrated treatment and recycling of stormwater: a review of Australian practice, *Journal of Environmental Management*, 79: 102–113.

Jalil, M.A. and Njiru, C. (2006) '*Water Demand Management in Urban Water Supplies – Present and Future Challenges*', in Rahman, M.M., Bin Alam, M.J., Ali, M.A. and Smout, I. (eds), Environmental Sustainability Concerns, pp.43-57, Environmental Engineering Division (EED), Centre for Environmental and Resource Management (CERM), and International Training Network (ITN) Centre, Bangladesh University of Engineering and Technology, Dhaka, Bangladesh.

Rauner, M.S. and Schaffhauser-Linzatti, M, (2002) Impact of the new Austrian inpatient payment strategy on hospital behaviour: a system-dynamics model, *Socio-Economic Planning Sciences*, 36: 161–182.

Renwick, M.E. and Green, R.D. (2000) Do Residential Water Demand Side Management Policies Measure Up? An Analysis of Eight California Water Agencies, *Journal of Environmental Economics and Management*, 40: 37-55.

Savenije, H. and van der Zaag, P. (2002) Water as an economic good and demand management: paradigms with pitfalls, *Water International*, 27 (1): 98-104.

Turner, A., Willets, J., Fane, S., Guirco, D., Kazaglis, A., and White, S. (2006) Planning our future urban water resources: A guide to demand management in the context of integrated resource planning, Institute of Sustainable Futures, University of Technology, Sydney.

UN-HABITAT (2009) *Planning sustainable cities: global report on human settlements*, Nairobi.

Van Rooijen, D., H. Turral, H. and Biggs, T.W. (2005) '*Sponge City: Water Balance of mega-city water use and wastewater use in Hyderabad, India.*' Irrigation and Drainage 54: 81-91.

VENSIM (1998) The Ventana Simulation Environment, VENSIM PLE Plus Version 5.3a. Copyright 1988-2003 Ventana Systems, Inc.

Von Medeazza, G.M. and Moreau, V. (2007) Modelling of water–energy systems: The case of desalination, *Energy*, 32: 1024–1031.

White, S.B. and Fane, S.A. (2001) Designing Cost Effective Water Demand Management Programs in Australia, *Water Science and Technology* 46 (6-7): 225-232.

Yeh, S., Wang, C, and Yu, H.(2006) Simulation of soil erosion and nutrient impact using an integrated system dynamics model in a watershed in Taiwan, *Environmental Modelling & Software*, 21: 937-948.

5

Agent-based Modelling for Demand Side Water Management Strategies

Seneshaw Tsegaye and Kala Vairavamoorthy

Introduction

The continuously intensifying scarcity of water resources is a crucial problem in almost all contemporary societies. The traditional methods emphasize increasing water supplies, but do not consider water consumption reduction. However, under the scarcity of water resources and financial constraints, promoting people's awareness towards reduction of water consumption, changing the habits of water use, and improving water use efficiency should be taken into account. The demand management paradigm has emerged to influence and reshape demand by mechanisms such as metering, initiatives such as water recycling and the promotion of water-saving technologies. However, studies on the role of social networks and non-tariff-based techniques for water conservation are in their infancy (Rixon, and Burn, 2002).

This work aims to develop an Agent Based Model (ABM) to capture the complex interaction between water stakeholders for estimation of residential water demand and to explore an optimum demand side water management strategy. The model is composed of interacting consumers, water supplier, and policy maker "agents". The model also introduces inter agent communication to simulate the dynamic behaviour of actual consumers through an influence diffusion mechanism.

The model can simulate the residential water demand–supply chain and analyze impacts of the factors on residential water consumption. It can be used for choosing a cost effective urban water management strategy. It also provides makers with a useful tool to evaluate water price policies and non-tariff based techniques for water conservation in different options. The model development was done using C++ programming language. Semi-hypothetical tests of the model have been done to determine the residential water consumption and assess the performance of alternative demand-side management policy instruments in terms of their effectiveness in reducing aggregate demand and their distribution implication.

Literature review

Water demand management

Water Demand Management (WDM) practices are crucial for shifting the orientation of urban water policy towards a more sustainable direction. They require integration of engineering, environment and socio-economic aspects of water management. Traditionally, municipal water utilities have taken a reactive approach to providing adequate supplies to meet the needs of residential, industrial, and other water users. Increased demand typically has been met via construction of new plants and the establishment of new sources of supply. However, WDM should involve a broad range of measures that aim to increase the efficiency of water use. These can include:

- conservation-oriented tariff structures
- public awareness campaigns
- pressure management and leak reduction programs
- water audits
- water saving and reuse technologies.

The effectiveness of WDM policy instruments in increasing efficiency and their equity implications for residential users is a debated issue among economists and policy makers (Renwick, and Archibald, 1998). For example economists generally advocate higher water prices as a major WDM option; others argue that non-price policies, which directly control residential water use, are the only viable means to reduce water demand. For example Arbués et al., (2003) suggest water price as the main instrument to control demand. Other scholars argue that all WDM activities will directly or indirectly affect consumers and hence a public awareness campaign will play an important role in any WDM programme (Vairavamoorthy and Mansoor, 2006).

According to Renwick and Archibald (1998), one of the problems facing policy makers and water utility managers is lack of adequate information and appropriate tools to determine the performance of price and non-price policy instruments. This suggests the need to develop a new methodology and appropriate tools that can capture the impact of different WDM instruments in reducing the consumption of water. Moreover, the decision-making process in urban water management should include all water stakeholders. Coordination between various water agencies and enforcement bodies has major advantages in planning an effective water conservation policy. It also promotes decentralization and participation of stakeholders so as to broaden the role of the civil society in water management.

In recent years it has also become increasingly evident that the human dimension plays a key role in resources management (Pahl-Wostl and Hare, 2004). Ensuring communication and exchange of information and knowledge are decisive factors for providing enduring and socially acceptable solutions. This requires that WDM policies are focused towards using social influence to reduce consumption in residential areas. Social modelling in WDM was taken into account in a new approach that simulates the diffusion of information through the interaction between water consumers. Thus, determining optimal WDM policies should implement an appropriate modelling tool and methodology which can simulate the dynamic interactions between all water stakeholders. Renwick and Archibald, (1998) highlight the advantage of the ABM approach over the other equation based approaches in building dynamic interactions of the real world. Moss et al., (2001) also propose that agent-based social simulation supports a methodology that itself provides a suitable framework for collecting observations of the social and physical systems, to identify relationships and processes. ABMs, due to their inherent characteristics, can be effectively used to model both the dynamics and the complexity of WDM. Therefore, in this work an ABM tool is developed and applied for exploring optimal demand-side management strategy.

Agent based modelling

ABM is a powerful simulation modelling technique that has seen a number of applications in the last few years, including applications to real-world problems. It competes with equation-based approaches in many disciplines. According to Parunak et al., (1998) the forms of the model and the way that it executes the relationships are the major differences between agent-based and equation-based approaches. In ABM, the model consists of a set of agents that encapsulate the behaviours of the various individuals that make up the system, and the execution consists of emulating these behaviours. However in equation-based modelling, the model is a set of equations, and execution consists of evaluating them.

In the real world, there are many systems that are too complex and large to be captured by a single agent. So Xu et al. (2008) suggested that with a multi-agent modelling approach it is possible to deal with entities at different ranges of complexity and unity. Multi-Agent Systems comprise multiple agents, which interact among themselves or with objects in their environment, having a limited viewpoint and in the absence of a system global control point. They try to represent complex systems by defining the involved entities (individual or collective) and by formulating their behaviour and interaction in the specific environment.

The fundamental idea behind agent-based models is that decision-making is distributed among autonomous actors, which either operate individually or may communicate (Laine, 2006). ABMs have multiple applications but we are particularly interested in modelling the dynamic interaction between water stakeholders to determine the residential water demand. The water consumer agent (CA), water supplier agent (WSA) and policy maker agent (PMA) are used to represent the interacting water stakeholders.

Agent based models for water management

Agent-based models have successfully been applied to water management problems, thus, showing the great potential for future decision support development. For instance, the Freshwater Integrated Resource Management with Agents (FIRMA) project has used an agent-based model for the simulation of physical, hydrological, social and economic aspects of water resource management. It improves existing integrated assessments by explicitly representing customers, suppliers, and government and their interaction at various levels of aggregation. FIRMA yields insights into the social processes of water management, leading to the consideration of a wider range of aspects of the environment in decision-making. FIRMA is a decision support tool for the integrated design of water management.

The other example is DAWN, a software tool for evaluating water-pricing policies, where a multi-agent system is implemented to simulate the residential water demand-supply chain. An agent community is assigned to behave as water consumers, while econometric and social models are incorporated into them for estimating water consumption. DAWN's main advantage is that it supports social interaction between consumers, through an influence diffusion mechanism, implemented via inter-agent communication (Athanasiadis et al, 2004). It enables the design, creation, modification and execution of different options for policy making.

Rixon and Burn, (2002) formulated ABMs to investigate the effects of social networks, tariff structures, technology adoption and water use behaviour on water conservation. The model output shows social networks result in a significant reduction in simulated water use under the variable tariff regime and this suggests that within small communities where social cohesion is strong, there is ability for non-tariff-based strategies to successfully impact on water use.

In this work, we adopt an agent based approach to deal with the complexities derived from multiple factors which influence the domestic water consumption. This paper also describes the development and application of a simple agent-based model to explore the effects of social networks and tariff structures on water use behaviour.

ABM formulation for residential water demand

Residential demand forecast model

According to Kolokytha et al,, (2002) the investigation of the determination of the residential water demand is a prerequisite for any demand-driven water policy design. For estimating residential water demand, a variety of methods and econometric models have been used on the basis of the nature and availability of data, for example:

$$Q(i, t) = a + bP(i, t) + cH(i) + \xi(i, t) \dots\dots\dots\dots\dots\dots\dots (1)$$

Where

- $Q(i, t)$ is the water consumption for household i at time t ;
- $P(i, t)$ is the vector of price variables;
- $H(i)$ is a vector of household and community-specific variables;
- a, b, c are coefficients to be estimated (elasticities);
- $\xi(i, t)$ is the error term.

Social model

In the water demand supply chain all members of the area consumer society interacts with each other. To simulate this social interaction we adopt the mechanism used by (Athanasiadis et al, 2005).

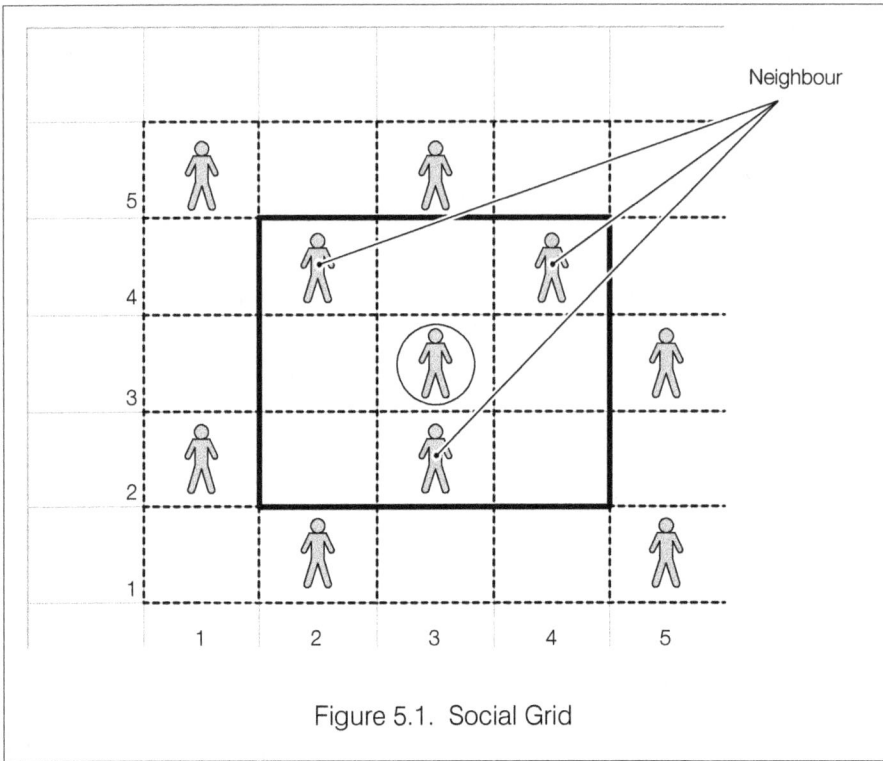

Figure 5.1. Social Grid

A 2-D social grid shown in Figure 5.1 is used to simulate the society of consumer agent (CA), whose communication represents social relationship among them. Each CA is determined by its position on the social grid. So, a single CA is defined as CA(x, y), where x, and y are its coordinates on the grid. The social interaction between CAs is limited to neighbourhood. As an example consider CA (3, 3) in Figure 5.1 shown above. If the neighbourhood scope is limited to 1, then the neighbourhood area of CA (3, 3) is marked out by the square frame. As the figure demonstrates the water consumption of CA (3, 3) is affected only by its three neighbours CA (2, 4), CA (3, 2) and CA (4, 4). The neighbouring agents communicate their Social Weight (Sw) that represents their ability to persuade.

Consumers' ability to change their water demand depends not only on the influence of neighbours but also on consumers' own attitude to reduce water consumption (comprehending ability). The social function is, therefore, defined as a function of promoting ability of neighbours and comprehending ability of consumers.

$$S(i, t) = f (Cw , \sum 1ni\ Swij) \dots\dots\dots\dots\dots\dots\dots\dots\dots\dots\dots(2)$$

Where

- S(i, t) is the social variable of CAi at time t,
- Swij is the social weight that consumer agent CAi receives from its neighbour j, it depends on neighbours' ability to promote conservation signal;
- ni is the number of neighbours of CAi.
- Cw is a function for adjusting the sum of social weights, and it represents a consumers' ability to comprehend water conservation signals.

In this model the analysis of the extent to which price policies, non price demand management options and their combination reduce residential water consumption is done through option evaluation. The economic model is then implemented in the code to evaluate the influence of alternative WDM policy instruments (such as water saving technology, public education) and increasing block pricing schedules.

In order to consider the social influence the modified econometric model $Q= f(P, H, S)$, which is suggested by Athanasiadis et al, (2005) is used.

$$Q(i, t) = a + bP(i, t) + cH(i) + dS(i, t) + \xi(i, t) \dots\dots\dots\dots (3)$$

Where S(i, t) is the vector of social attribute variables.

ABM structure

In agent based modeling of residential water demand the systems that need to be analyzed and modelled are more complex in terms of their interdependencies (Macal and North, 2005). The structure of this multi-agent based model includes three kinds of agents: water consumer agent (CA), water supplier agent (WSA) and policy maker agent (PMA).

Agent role

Consumer agent

CA plays the major role in the simulation. It encapsulates the dynamic behaviour for area residents who consume water and pick up its cost. This agent also sends complaints to PMA if they are not happy with the water tariff and unable to get basic consumption due to the price placed on water usage. The actual consumers interact with each other and this social activity is one of the major factors which affect water consumption behaviour. Thus, in this study a social interaction model is incorporated to define the dynamic consumer behaviour. CA communicates with neighbours to propagate demand management and price policy. In this model the influence of the neighbours' over the consumers' attitude is reflected through social weight. The influence mechanism is shown on page 82.

Water supply agent

WSA advises water price to PMA according to its benefit. This agent is responsible for billing CAs for their consumption and calculates the total demand. WSA also complains to PMA if they lose their revenue and maximum consumption is exceeded.

Policy maker agent

The fundamental decisions, such as the determination of investments in water sector and water tariff structures, have been strongly influenced by administrative rationale (Arbués, et al., 2003). Furthermore, in water management strategy, demand analysis is a precondition of designing an optimum socioeconomic water use and the respective water price. In this model setup PMA enacts price policy depending on the information received from the CAs and WSA at different time steps revises it in timely fashion.

Social function

In addition to meeting consumers demand, water strategies generally have to discourage reckless waste by encouraging a 'wise use' attitude. Calls for the public to save water over many years have made them value water and become very conservation conscious. Recorded questionnaire data about consumers' interaction and motives to conserve water, and direct observation data of individual water consumption reduction due to implementation of water conservation education/campaign are used to generate the social model. This social function is then used as an input for our model.

The model adopts survey results from the city of Thessaloniki, Greece by Kolokytha et al,. (2002). Consumer agents are clustered in four types based on their ability to promote and comprehend water-conserving information, as shown in Table 5.1.

Table 5.1 Consumer type			
Consumer type		Ability to promote	Ability to comprehend
A	Opinion leaders	High	Low
B	Socially apathetic	None	None
C	Opinion seekers	Low	High
D	Opinion receivers	Low	Low

According to their ability to promote water conservation signals:

- Type A: Opinion leaders are promoters of the conservation signals and are supposed to influence their neighbours. They have high ability to promote.

- Type B: Socially apathetic, insensitive to social issues and don't promote water saving signals

- Type C: Opinion seekers; are socially sensitive but have low ability to promote water conservation signals.

- Type D: Opinion receivers; are average consumers who have low ability to promote water conservation signals.

Agent based model simulation modules

This ABM is developed by consideration of multiple interacting agents - consumers, water suppliers and policy makers. At each simulation step the agents interact at different levels to determine the appropriate tariff structure and demand management strategy. The developed ABM is used to improve the understanding of how different demand-side water management policies are expected to influence consumption of different classes of residential household. This model is composed of two large modules having independent tasks: Tariff Structure Simulation and Option Evaluation.

Tariff structure simulation

The first module is constructed in the model to determine the suitable price block structure. In this module, consumer, water supplier and policy maker agents interact at each simulation step to determine an appropriate tariff structure. The interaction between all agents is mediated by the policymaker. At each step the policy maker receives information from all consumers and suppliers to decide on the modification of the tariff structure (i.e. an increase or reduction of unit prices).

In this model setup a three-block initial tariff structure is implemented as an input. The first block price is for satisfying the basic consumption need of consumers and the tariff related to this block is set to remain constant. The other two price blocks however, will be varied during simulation based on the information received through the interaction of consumer, supplier and policy maker agents. The policy maker agent varies the tariffs until it converges to a point where consumer and supplier agents accept the modified tariff structure.

Option evaluation

The ultimate effect of the demand-side management policies depend on the policy instrument selected and the composition of aggregate demand. The extent to which a particular policy instrument reduces aggregate demand equals the sum of the savings from individual households. The option evaluation module of this ABM examines alternative demand-side water conservation policy instruments such as conservation-oriented tariff structures, social network / public awareness campaigns, water reuse and saving technologies etc...

The social influence is one of the key drivers on water use behaviour of consumers and needs further detailed studies. This module of the model is constructed in such a way that it can capture the actual dynamic behaviour of consumers and the diffusion of social influence within the consumer agents. The simulation of this module is performed under any initial input tariff structure and other demand management options with different policy review schedules to evaluate and choose the most effective one.

Model simulation procedure

Tariff structure simulation steps

The model simulates the interaction of consumer, water supplier and policy maker agents to suggest a suitable tariff structure and determine residential water demand. An abstract description of the model simulation procedure involves the following steps:

- users prepare the initial input parameters such as water demand econometric model, population size and growth rate, neighbourhood limit etc..
- WSA initializes water tariff structure.

- PMA enact the price and informs both WSA and CAs.
- CA receives price information, and communicates with its neighbours according to the social influence mechanism.
- each CA estimates its own water demand. This step takes in to account consumer agent communication with each other.
- CA reports its water demand to WSA and any complaints to PMA.
- WSA collects all residents' demands, calculates the total consumption, total costs, and reports the results to PMA.
- PMA adjusts the price block structure if needed, (refer to the Option Evaluation Step 2 below).
- when the iteration is over, the model presents revised block tariff structure and the residential consumption.

Option evaluation steps

After the tariff structure iteration is performed the model simulates the residential water demand supply chain to determine an optimum demand-side water management option. The steps include:

1. Initialization and Option input

   Users prepare the simulation option by specifying a set of parameters for the demand-side management policy instruments. This include simulation duration, simulation step, demand management option to be simulated and policy review steps.

2. Model Simulation

   The model simulates the option entered by the users. During simulation all autonomous agents interact to determine the residential consumption within the time step. Each step simulates a time interval, during which water consumption is estimated.

3. Option Evaluation

   The model Option results are then evaluated by the user. From different simulation results users can make a comparison and decide on the optimum demand-side management strategy.

Model application and hypothetical test

Key data used

Social data
The social weight has to be assigned to consumers based on their ability

to promote and comprehend water conserving. However due to lack of this information we use an arbitrary social data and function shown in Tables 5.2. and 5.3.

Table 5.2. Social weight based on neighbours' ability to promote water conservation signal (Swij)			
Consumers		Relative Weight	Normalized
A	Opinion Leader	3W	1
B	Opinion Receiver	2W	2/3
C	Opinion Seeker	1W	1/3
D	Socially Apathetic	0W	0

Table 5.3. Social weight based on consumer ability to comprehend water conservation signal (Cwi)			
Consumers		Weight	Normalized
A	Opinion Leader	4	0.27
B	Opinion Receiver	7	0.88
C	Opinion Seeker	10	0.99
D	Socially Apathetic	1	0.02

The normalized weight value in Table 5.3, based on the ability to comprehend, is used as a modifying factor for the consumption reduction due to social influence of neighbours. Therefore, in this semi hypothetical test, the social function is defined randomly as:

$$S(i, t) = -0.2(1+Cwi) \sum Swij.$$

Experiment simulation options

The ABM can address a broad range of options to explore an optimum demand management strategy. In this hypothetical test, the model was used to evaluate four options, which are as follows:

- Option 1: water price is adjusted to the real price, without public social education. (Assumed inflation 5%)

- Option 2: water price is increased by 10%, without public social education.

- Option 3: water price is adjusted to the real price, with the implementation of education or other information policy.

- Option 4: water price is increased by 10%, with the implementation of education or other information policy.

Results

Tariff iteration outputs

From an initial stepped tariff structure the policy maker agent receives information from both water supply and consumer agents at each tariff iteration step and changes the price tariff if necessary. Figure 5.2 shows the resulting variation of price values to determine an appropriate water tariff.

Based on the response of all interacting agents, the model suggested the price tariff structure shown in Figure 5.3, below. This modified price block can be used as an input for option evaluation step or different input tariff structure can be used.

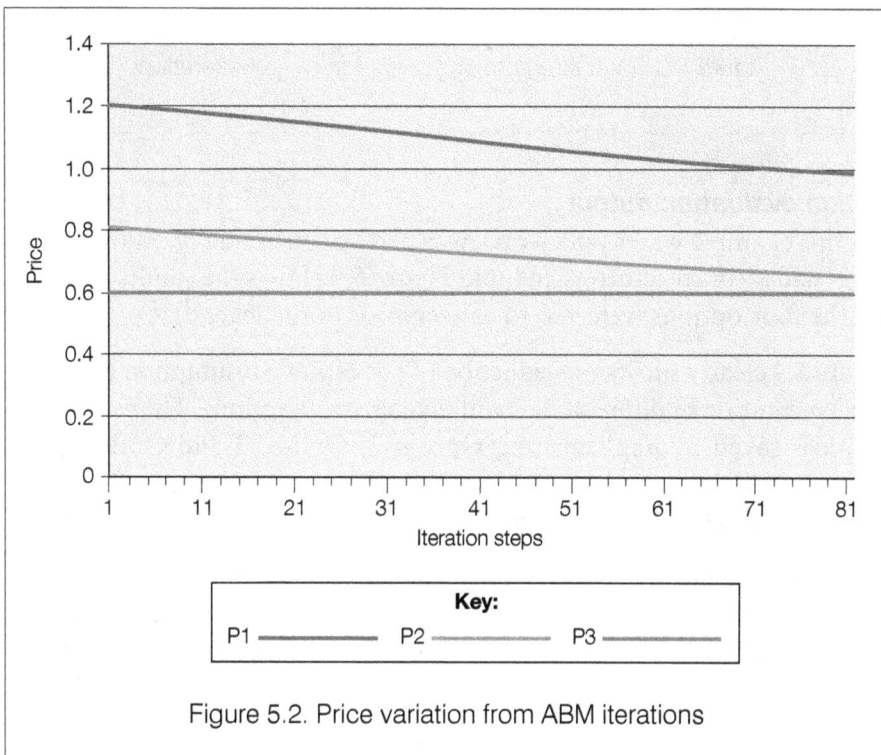

Figure 5.2. Price variation from ABM iterations

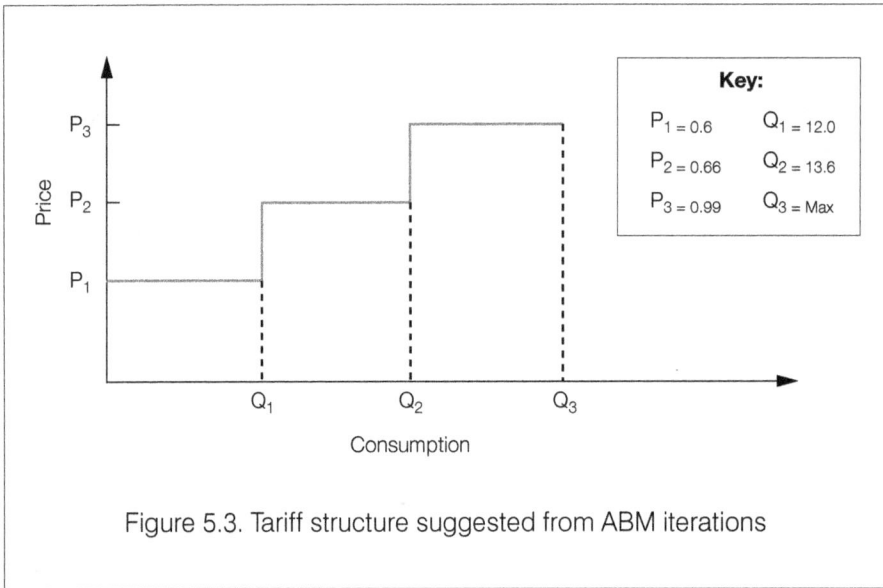

Figure 5.3. Tariff structure suggested from ABM iterations

Option evaluation output

For this example water policy review is performed annually. Adopting the suggested tariff structure as an input Figure 5.4 shows the results obtained for the four options (referred to as scenarios in the legend).

Figure 5.4 clearly shows the reduction of per capita consumption under the implementation of different demand management options. The cumulative volumes saved by implementing Option 2, Option 3 and Option 4 are about 8.7%, 9.2% and 16.2 % respectively at the end of the simulation (48 months) when compared to Option 1.

Interestingly, Option 4 on Figure 5.4 shows an initial reduction of consumption followed by a small increment after simulation duration of 36 months. This is because the consumption reduction by some consumers gives an opportunity to reduce their expense. Thus, the reduction in expense allows some consumers to shift from small consumption to large consumption block, which in turn increase the average per capita consumption.

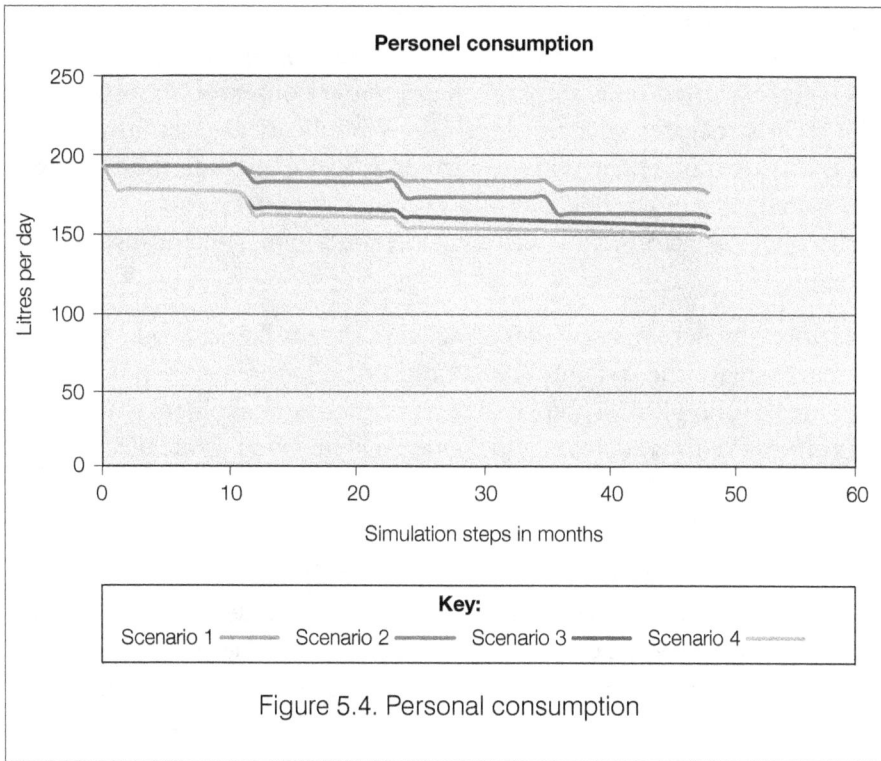

Figure 5.4. Personal consumption

Conclusion and recommendations

In this work we develop an Agent Based Model for estimation of residential water demand under different water management strategies. This Agent Based Model captures and shows the pattern of residential consumption and how it is changing with the change in behaviour of consumers as a result of different decisions (such as change in water tariff structure, implementation of public awareness/education) made by autonomous bodies such as water utilities or regulators. The model emulates the real social interaction within consumers and gives an opportunity to explore the effect of information-diffusion in reducing residential water demand. Thus, it can be used effectively by decision-makers to evaluate different water conservation options and chose an optimum demand-side management strategy. In addition to evaluate different water conservation options, the model is used to suggest the water tariff structure that is appropriate for both water consumers and supply authorities. This offers further opportunity for regulators to monitor the tariff structure set by water utilities.

Demand-side management involves a broad range of measures that aim to increase the efficiency of water use but due to limitation of time and lack of information/data, only the major water conservation instruments such tariff structures and social influence (public awareness/information diffusion) are implemented in the current model. However, the developed tool is an open source code that allows coupling with existing models and further extension to include different demand management instruments if required.

Therefore, the developed model is a generic Agent Based Model tool that can encapsulate the dynamic behaviours of all water stakeholders and simulate the complex response patterns of these stakeholders with a view to exploring optimal demand side water management strategies.

Acknowledgment

This work is a part of the research by WEDC: Water Engineering Development Centre at Loughborough University funded by the SWITCH: Managing Water for the City of the Future program. The authors gratefully acknowledge support from the SWITCH grant that has made this work possible. We also thank Loughborough University for giving support in achieving the outputs.

References

Arbues, F., Garcia-Valinas, M. ı. A. & Martinez-Espineira, R. (2003). Estimation of residential water demand: a state-of-the-art review. *Journal of Socio-Economics*, 32, 81–102.

Athanasiadis, I. N., Vartalas, P. & Mitkas, P. A. (2004) DAWN: A platform for evaluating water-pricing policies using a software agent society. In: *International Environmental Modelling and Software Society (iEmSs 2004) Complexity and Integrated Resources Management,14-17 June, 2004, University of Osnabruck, Germany.*

Athanasiadis, I. N., Mentes, A. K., Mitkas, P. A. & Mylopoulos, Y. A. (2005). A hybrid Agent-Based Model for estimating residential water demand. SIMULATION: Transactions of the Society for Modeling and Simulation Interanational, 81, 189-199.

Kolokytha, E. G., Mylopoulos, Y. A. & Mentes, A. K. 2002. Evaluating demand management aspects of urban water policy—A field survey in the city of Thessaloniki, Greece. *Urban Water*, 4, 391–400.

Laine, T. (2006) *Agent-based model selection framework for complex adaptive systems*. PhD thesis, Computer Science and Cognitive Science, Indiana University.

Macal, C. M. & North, M. J. 2005 Tutorial on Agent-Based Modeling and Simulation. In: *Proceedings of the Winter Simulation Conference, December 4-7, 2005, Orlando, Florida*

Moss, S.; Pahl-Wostl, C. & Downing, T. (2001) Agent-based integrated assessment modelling: the example of climate change. Integrated Assessment, 2, 17–30.

Mylopoulos, Y. A.; Mentes, A. K., & Theodossiou, I.(2004). Modeling Residential Water Demand Using Household Data: A Cubic Approach. *Water International*, 29(1), 105–113.

Olmstead, S. M. & Stavins, R. N. (2007). *Managing Water Demand Price vs. Non-Price Conservation Programs* (Pioneer Institute White Paper No 39). Pioneer Institute Public Policy Research, Boston, Massachusetts.

Parunak, H. V. D., Savit, R. & Riolo, R. L. (1998) Agent-Based Modeling vs. Equation-Based Modeling: A Case Study and Users' Guide. In: *Multi- Agent Systems and Agent-based Simulation, Proceedings of First International Workshop MABS*; '98, July 4-6, Paris, France.

Pahl-Wostl, C. and M. Hare (2004). Processes of Social Learning in Integrated Resources Management. *Journal of Community & Applied Social Psychology* 14, 193–206

Renwick, E. M. and S. O. Archibald (1998). Demand side management for residential water use: who bear the conservation burden? *Land Economics*. 74(3), 343-359

Rixon, A. & Burn, S. 2002. Exploring Water Conservation Behaviour Through Participatory Agent-Based Modelling. In: *IFAC, modelling and Control for Participatory Planning and Managing Water Systems*, 29 September, 2004, Venice, Italy.

Vairavamoorthy, K. and Mansoor, M.A.M. (2006). Demand management in developing countries. In: Butler, D. and Memon. F. A. (eds.) *Water Demand Management*. IWA Publishing, London, UK. pp. 180-214.

Xu, M, Hu, Z., Wu, J., and Zhou, Y. (2008) A hybrid society model for simulating residential electricity consumption. *Electrical Power and Energy Systems*, 30, 569–574.

6

Zoning Tool for Water Distribution Leakage Control

Jotham Sempewo, Assela Parthirana and Kala Vairavamoorthy

Introduction

More than half of the world's population live in urban centres where the only viable means of supplying water for consumption is by piped water systems. As described in Chapter 1, it is expected that in the year 2030 urban population will have increased to about 2 billion, with 95% of the increase coming from developing countries - which will worsen the existing water situation. Water distribution systems (WDS) in cities are continuously evolving to match the increase in demand arising from urban growth, change in consumption patterns, industrial development, etc. The need to meet the demand of the world's population has resulted in repeatedly modifying the existing system to meet demand. This has yielded highly complex looped interconnected systems that are complicated to partition for better management and yet partitioning these systems into discrete zones of manageable size has become a need of the day. What worsens the situation is that the existing designs were made without consideration that there would be segmentation in future (Deuerlein, 2006).

Existing water distribution efficiencies are further worsened by other factors such as poor distribution efficiency through city networks and inequalities in service provision between the rich and the poor. Typically, water loss in water supply systems ranges from 15% to 30% in the developed world but elsewhere it is likely to range from 30% to 60% (Bridges, 1994). The segmentation of water distribution networks into manageable areas or sectors called leakage control zones (LCZs) has therefore become a more and more pressing "must have" phenomenon that water companies are struggling to achieve for a better Non Revenue Water (NRW) control and reduction strategy. These zones or District Meter Areas (DMAs) could serve a variety of purposes like 1) Managing Unaccounted for Water (UFW), 2) Pressure regulation, 3) Asset management of WDS infrastructure (e.g. Renewal planning) and 4) Equitable supply of water during scarcity scenarios (possibly including rotation of supply).

Many water utility companies both in the developed and developing countries have adopted leakage monitoring as the best practice approach, and systematic techniques for estimation of losses within the zones have been developed. However the demarcating of the zones themselves still remains arbitrary, varies from country to country and mainly relies on local experience. Definition of the zonal boundaries is drawn from experience gained from existing practice and local knowledge (WHO, 2001). The zones are created on "paper" maps and then transferred into hydraulic models to predict their performance. In such an approach it is difficult to create optimal zones, for example in terms of number of flow meters required in the system or the time taken to locate a detected leak. Furthermore, this "try and see" approach is time consuming and costly before any reasonably good DMA zones are established. This has an implication for the cost of set up and maintenance of the zone, as well as for the effectiveness that can be achieved since the time run of a leak is one of the most important determinants of the amount of water loss.

Furthermore, the selected water demand management strategy is indiscriminately applied to the entire urban water distribution system, neglecting the fact that each of the potential DMA zones would be more suited for its own demand management strategy that recognizes its uniqueness. This calls for the creation of DMAs to allow for the application of appropriate intervention on specific areas based on the optimization of available resources. Currently there is no prototype optimal zoning and leakage control design tool for complicated water networks with the objective of monitoring UFW, minimizing leakage and for optimal control of network pressures. Above all there is no tool that makes the design methodology generic, repeatable, faster and replicable. By creating optimal DMAs, water loss in water distribution systems could be minimized. The water saved could then be used to improve performance, for example in developing countries to supply the un-served people where basic levels of service are not yet met. There is, therefore, a need to develop techniques that can facilitate the development of optimal LCZs in a systematic way.

This paper presents the development and testing of a water distribution zone demarcation tool as one of the tools that can be used by service providers to effectively manage demand in their water supply systems.

The approach proposes optimal zoning schemes for complicated water networks with the objective of monitoring unaccounted for water, which is one of the ways through which demand management can be achieved in the WDS. The approach uses the distributed computing analogy to distribute workloads among processors to suggest optimal zoning schemes for the networks.

The performance of the tool is demonstrated by its application on a few complicated networks. The tool can help water companies increase their productivities and also optimize resource allocations by reduction of the time to monitor, discover leaks and partition zones. In addition the tool can be used to enhance leakage reduction and monitoring given that the network will have been broken down into smaller components that can be monitored. The costs of the leakage identification and control exercise can also be greatly reduced once proper monitoring is done. System sectorizing helps facilitate easy identification of potential leakage hot spots in the distribution system which can act as an early indicator of system performance. It is thus a helpful tool in the prioritization of zones for more detailed assessment and study in light of often scarce resources, thereby helping the water industry to enhance the sustainability and equity of water supply.

The DMA Philosophy

The need for DMAs

According to the DMA design manual (Morrison et al., 2007), the philosophy that governs creation of DMAs is the use of flow to determine leakage level within a selected water distribution area. Monitoring flows entering and leaving a zone allows easy detection of new bursts and leakages which enables appropriate action to be taken at the optimum level. This philosophy aims to reduce the length of time of a leak given that: Burst leakage=(the rate of flow)x(the length of time over which the break/burst has occurred). Whereas significant reductions can be made, continuous monitoring and measures have to be carried out because leakage is not static but rather dynamic and is also dependent on the hydraulic characteristics of the WDS.

Partitioning of a water distribution system during the application and selection of an appropriate leakage management option enables the promotion of a more modular approach to leakage management. When the zones are created then meters can be placed at zone boundaries to measure flows into and out of the zone. It is these zone inflows (water supplied) that are balanced with the household meter readings (zone outflows or water consumed) with differences signifying water loss. Such information can be mapped onto a WDS pipe condition map to enable the prioritization of the zone for leakage interventions. Zones without any water loss are given less priority whereas those with high water losses are given immediate attention. In addition, leakage management interventions could depend on the difference between current leakage and the economic level of leakage. Created zones can also be used when selectively applying optimal leakage management strategies that respond to the water loss issues for every different zone. The optimal partitioning of a WDS is therefore undoubtedly the first task that has to be undertaken if different leakage management measures are to be applied to different zones for best results.

DMA sizing methodology

The objective of creating DMAs is to have manageable zones, however no clear definition has been made to define what is manageable. A DMA size has an impact on the cost of creating them. Currently size is limited to pipe length and number of connections. This can be quite a challenging task given that networks have varying topologies and characteristics which may be hard to group using such parameters. Yates and Donald (2005) recommended the maximum DMA size to be based on the acceptable leakage run time of 3 days. The researcher recommended the size of either, 150-200 hydrants, or 2500 connections, or 30 km of water main. Size ideally depends on the network being considered and on other factors like level of automation and the level of leakage.

Though the smaller the zone the more the set up costs, the benefits of small zones in the long run may exceed the set up cost. These benefits include better classification of a WDS network for improved management and application e.g. selective application of demand management approaches for easy identification of leaks due to a reduced area of coverage, reduction in location times, reduction in detection cost and ease in maintaining a lower leakage level (Morrison et al., 2007).

Methodologies for DMA prioritization for leakage detection.

The guiding principle for DMA prioritization is the selection of the best DMA that when worked on, will yield more benefits than the costs of detecting the leakage. (Morrison et al., 2007). A cost benefit analysis based on detection of additional repair costs, reduction of leakage level, value savings and a leakage return frequency should be carried out to prioritize the order of intervention to the DMAs. Currently the DMA concept lacks historical data given that it is a new concept being applied. In addition there are difficulties in calculating the value of leakage. To circumvent the said shortcomings simplistic methods which use parameters like leakage per unit length or connection are normally adopted. These methods are not reliable for systems with intermittent supplies, as found in the cities of many developing countries.

Prioritization can also be done on the basis of marginal savings and customer connections. The DMA with the highest ratio of R is selected first:

$$R = \frac{\text{Marginal value of savings (per m}^3\text{) x excess losses(m}^3\text{/ day)}}{\text{(No of customer connections)}}$$

There is also an indirect approach where excess leakage is converted into bursts which are later used to estimate the amount of resources required to reduce a given leakage volume. This is then used as a rank to prioritize the different zones (Morrison et al., 2007).The above mentioned principles will provide a methodology for sizing and prioritization of the DMAs.

The approach and zone demarcation tool

The approach

The approach uses the distributed computing analogy in distribution of workloads among processors to suggest optimal zoning schemes for complicated networks with the objective of monitoring unaccounted for water. Analogous to the distributed computing load distribution problem, the first process of the approach is the conversion of the water distribution network into a graph which is thereafter discretized into a finite dimensional space through coding data of the graph properties to form concrete elements which are equally distributed among the processors. On the other hand minimizing inter-processor communication is applied as a partitioning objective that minimizes the number of pipes that straddle two different zones. It is also analogous to minimization of the diameter and pipes put together, with minimization of pipe flows that straddle two zones. Various graph partitioning algorithms that have extensive application in parallel computing (Karypis and Kumar, 1995; Karypis and Kumar, 1995; Karypis et al., 1999) exist and are imported for application in the WDS graph partition problem.

First different single objectives are introduced which are later combined to form the multi-objective partitions. The basis for the zoning schemes are weights. The objectives are formulated from literature about DMA size determinants like connections or a specified length (Yates and Donald, 2005) which for the purposes of this study are simplified to represent demand and length respectively and are introduced into the model as arguments (weights). For the pipes the only weight assigned is diameter and for the nodes either demand or lengths are assigned as weights for formation of the single objective zoning scheme. A multi-objective zoning scheme is formed by combination of any of the single objectives mentioned above. In the zoning tool, balancing length or demand within the zones is achieved by assigning vectors to each node. The partitioning tool then partitions with the aim of fulfilling the balancing constraint associated with each zoning scheme while at the same time trying to minimize the pipes cut.

The tool

Based on the above approach a tool is developed with the Orange user interface written in the Python programming language. The structure of the developed model consists of the zone demarcation model and the zonal mass balance model. Details of the model, and the partitioning objectives together with the evaluation of the performance of the tools could be found in Sempewo et al. 2011. The tool is developed using C++, the METIS library and the EPANET tool kit. Visual C++ is used to code the geometrical information of the EPANET input file format into a graph which was passed on as an input to the METIS library partitioner. EPANET is used to compute the extended period simulations of the distribution system during the partitioning process from which weights are also generated. Details of the structure and flow charts of the developed model can be found in Sempewo et al. (2011).

The performance of the tool is demonstrated by its application on a few complicated networks and it was observed to be an efficient and effective approach for the optimal demarcation of complicated water networks into optimal zones based on balancing length, demand or flow within zones. This methodology can be applied to both systems under continuous supply and intermittent supply depending on the type of hydraulic solver used (pressure dependent or demand driven). The tool is never the less suited for continuous supply systems given that the hydraulic solver used (EPANET) is not pressure dependent but rather demand driven.

Examples

The developed zoning tool was also applied on large real case complex networks accessed from the Centre for Water Systems (2009). An example is shown in Figure 6.1 where the partition was based on minimizing the numbers of pipes cut, which in real terms means minimizing the number of meters at boundaries and the associated excavation etc. The process was efficient and the tool produced good results.

An alternative solution is shown in Figure 6.2, with the objective of minimizing the communication volume, i.e. the volume flowing across zone boundaries.

The tool and approach have also been applied elsewhere in a zone in Kampala Water to create leakage control zones for prioritization (Mujuni, 2010).

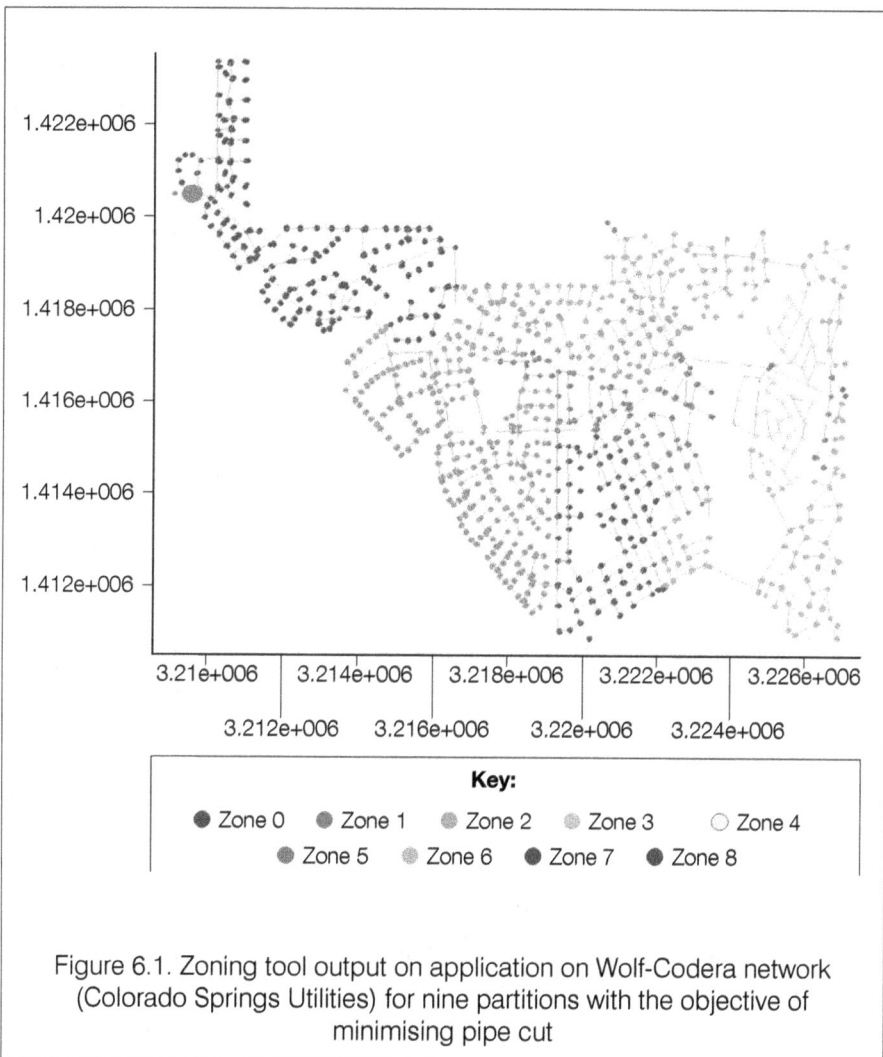

Figure 6.1. Zoning tool output on application on Wolf-Codera network (Colorado Springs Utilities) for nine partitions with the objective of minimising pipe cut

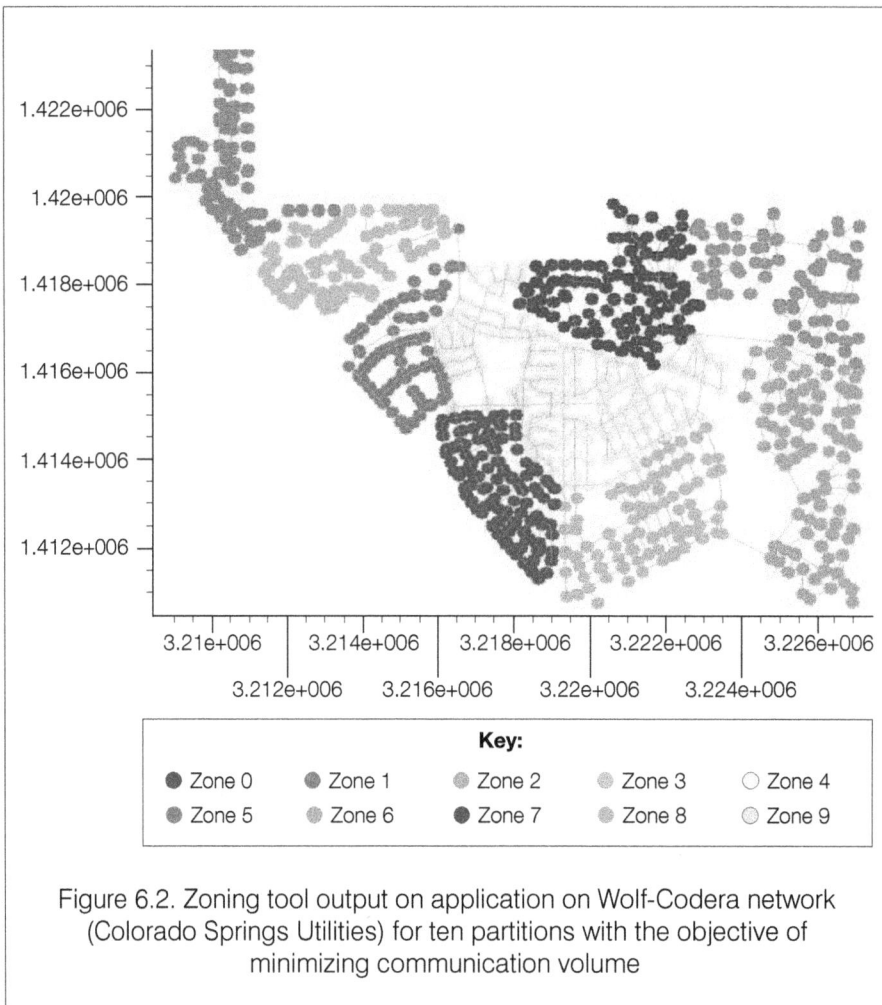

Figure 6.2. Zoning tool output on application on Wolf-Codera network
(Colorado Springs Utilities) for ten partitions with the objective of
minimizing communication volume

Practical application by water practitioners

The spatial analysis tool can be applied to a real world problem. In this section, an overview of the applicability of the tool on a case is presented. It begins with selection of a suitable study area, field data collection, building a hydraulic model and the estimation of the leakage in a network which could potentially be used to prioritize the leakage control zones.

Selection of typical study area

First and foremost, identify an urban water distribution system for which the tool is going to be applied. The identified area should be independent or hydraulically isolated from the main supply network to form a representative zone e.g. by having water entering the whole system flowing by gravity from a tank. This will allow better analysis and measurement of the pressure and flow profiles. The area has to be big enough so that it can hypothetically be divided into different leakage control zones later in the analysis.

Model input data collection

After isolating the study area network, the area's hydraulic performance is monitored by, for example, installing flow meters and pressure data loggers, to obtain actual field data. Accurate measurement of pressure and effective metering of continuous system inflow is ensured for proper network monitoring, and for development and calibration of the network model. Pressure readings could then be taken at strategic locations in the network so as to capture the average critical zones and critical points following the terrain of the area. These could either be near the inflow point i.e. tank, somewhere in the middle of the network or further downstream of the network supply point. It is encouraged that data collection for the network using data logging is performed at rotationally different points for say ten continuous days during which general supply reliability is good. The comprehensive field data that should be collected and recorded are summarized below:

- Urban water distribution system size and demand patterns e.g. number of customer connections or properties, different consumption categories like domestic, industrial, public standpipe, etc, number of connections in each consumption category, metered consumption from billing data.

- Specific urban water distribution system characteristic input data e.g. pipe lengths, pipe diameter, pipe material, pipe age, reported number of leaks and bursts in study area, total water consumption for the properties in the area, junction (nodal) elevation from contour maps, co-ordinates of network benchmarks.

- Specific urban water distribution system hydraulic data e.g. inlet point pressure, average and critical point pressure, system inlet flow.

Creating an input file and determination of number of zones

The calibrated network file in EPANET is then exported to create an input file for the tool of the format .inp. The number of zones to be created is dependent on length and numbers of properties/households served i.e. number of connections or length of water mains. If the total length of the network is X km and the desired length of pipes in a zone is Y km, then the number of zones shall be X/Y.

Note: The input file and the number of zones are the inputs to the model. The outputs are the pipes upon which metering devices can be placed.

Hydraulic modelling and leakage estimation

Using the field data collected about the study area network, a hydraulic model is built using EPANET 2 software (Rossman, 2000). The constructed model is calibrated by taking actual field measurements and altering the model parameters to match it to real life situation as much as possible. Pressure adjustment and demand adjustment is undertaken to calibrate the model. Zones are then created that depend on length and numbers of properties/households served i.e. number of connections or length of water mains.

For this purpose, suitable points within the network were identified for taking the actual field measurements. Furthermore the model should be verified for extended period simulation of the diurnal system profile by comparing the observed and calculated pressure and flow at the selected critical points, for example, at the inlet point over a period of time i.e. 12-48 hours depending on the reliability of flow. This calibration procedure should be repeated when taking care of the estimated leakage.

Leakage estimation and zone intervention prioritization

Leakage could either be measured from minimum night flow or on the other hand it could also be estimated from distribution within the system assuming it is considered as pressure-dependent demand. To explore opportunities for prioritization specific to a particular network, the system characteristics of the created zones should be analysed in detail - these include total pipe lengths in each created zone, total number of connections in each zone, total customer consumption in each zone and number of reported leakages and bursts in each zone. After estimating and/or determining leakage per zone from the mass balance it could be distributed depending on a few system characteristics like length, connections, demand, length etc. Given that the objective is to focus efforts on zones that would result in the biggest benefits a DMA prioritization methodology is selected based on the calculated leakage values and results of application of leakage zoning scheme. This could be the leakage value per length of pipe in a zone that offers the best benefits to the Utility.

Conclusion

A new water distribution zone demarcation method is presented that uses the analogy of graph partitioning principles used in distributed computing to distribute workloads among processors to suggest optimal zoning schemes based on balancing length, demand or flow within zones with the objective of monitoring of unaccounted for water.

Test cases and case studies are presented to demonstrate how the zoning tool is applied to the zone demarcation problem for the developed zoning schemes. The developed zone demarcation tool was observed to be an efficient and effective approach for the optimal demarcation of complicated water networks into optimal zones based on balancing length, demand or flow within zones. The tool is however sensitive to the number of partitions, the topology of the water distribution network and the partitioning algorithms used. The tool can be used as a decision support tool for the optimal development and reduction of uncertainties in development of leakage control zones by decision makers. This will enable water companies to increase their productivities and also optimise resource allocations by reduction of the time to monitor, discover leaks and partition zones. This will lead to improved operating revenues.

References

Centre for Water Systems (2007). Benchmarks. University of Exeter, UK, http://centres.exeter.ac.uk/cws/benchmarks [accessed 19 January 2011]

Deuerlein, J. (2006) Efficient Supply Network management based on Linear Graph Theory. In: *8th Annual Water Distribution Symposium, Cincinnati, Ohio, USA, August 27-30.*

Karypis, G., Aggarwal, R., Kumar, V., and Shekhar, S. (1999) Multilevel hypergraph partitioning: applications in VLSI domain. Very Large Scale Integration (VLSI) Systems, IEEE Transactions on, 7(1), 69-79.

Karypis, G., and Kumar, V. (1995a) Analysis of multilevel graph partitioning, ACM Press New York, NY, USA.

Kumar, V. (1995b) MeTis: Unstructured Graph Partitioning and Sparse Ordering System, Version 4.0. University of Minnesota, June.

Karypis, G., and Kumar, V. (1998) hMeTis: A hypergraph partitioning package.

Karypis, G., and Kumar, V. (1998) Multilevel algorithms for multi-constraint graph partitioning, IEEE Computer Society Washington, DC, USA.

Karypis, G., and Kumar, V. (1998c) Multilevel k-way Partitioning Scheme for Irregular Graphs. *Journal of Parallel and Distributed Computing*, 48(1), 96-129.

Morrison, J., Tooms, S., and Rogers, D. (2007) DMA Management Guidance Notes. International Water Association – Water Loss Task Force.

Mujuni, H. (2010) Application of Network Hydraulic Modelling for Leakage Management in Kampala City, Uganda MSc thesis (IUE-2008-10), Unesco-IHE, Delft, The Netherlands.

Rossman, L.A., (2000). EPANET 2 User's Manual, National Risk Management Research Laboratory, Office of research and Development, USEPA, EPA Publication EPA/600/R-00/057, September, 2000.

Sempewo, J., Parthirana, A. and Vairavamoorthy, K (2011) Development of a Water Distribution Leakage Control Zoning Tool from the Analogy of Distributed Computing. Unpublished Research Report, SWITCH

WHO (2001) Leakage Management and Control - A Best Practice Training Manual.

Yates, C. D., and Donald, G. M. (2005) DMA Design and Implementation, a North American Context. Leakage 2005.

Part 3

Implementing Water Demand Management: selected instruments and case studies

7

Partnership for water demand management at the end use level - case study of Zaragoza, Spain

Sam Kayaga, Laurent Sainctavit, Ian Smout and Victor Bueno

This paper was first presented at the International Water Association (IWA) Congress in Vienna, September 2008

Introduction

Need for integrated urban water resources management approaches

While the population in many industrialized countries is either decreasing or constant, the population in most developing countries is increasing rapidly, resulting in an overall global population increase. The most recent UN world population prospects report in July 2007 estimated that the global population reached 6.7 billion, 5.4 billion of which live in developing countries (United Nations, 2007). But the water resources have not only remained constant but have increasingly been polluted by the growing population. The rate of abstraction of freshwater has grown rapidly in tandem with human population growth. Consequently, per capita water availability is steadily declining. The water scarcity situation is compounded by the major impacts of climate change on the water resources, and the practical distribution problems concerned with time, space and affordability, leading to a widening gap between demand and supply in many parts of the world.

According to UN-HABITAT, 2007 was a historical year in which the proportion of people living in the worlds' urban areas hit the 50% mark (UN-HABITAT, 2006). The water scarcity situation will escalate in the urban areas where it is projected there will be a population increase of 2.12 billion people between 2000 and 2030, 95% of which will occur in developing countries (UN-HABITAT, 2004). The situation calls for the adoption of integrated urban water resources management (IUWRM). The principal components of IUWRM are supply optimization; demand management; participatory approaches to ensure equitable distribution; improved policy, regulatory and institutional framework; and an intersectoral approach to decision-making (UNEP-International Environmental Technology Centre, 2003).

Demand management (DM), one of the IUWRM components, may be defined as the development and implementation of strategies, policies, measures or other initiatives aimed at influencing demand, so as to achieve efficient and sustainable use of the scarce water resource (Savenije and van der Zaag, 2002). DM contrasts with the conventional supply-driven approach to water resources management, whose response to the ever increasing water demand is development of new water sources. There are five major categories of DM measures (White and Fane, 2001): those measures that (i) increase system efficiency at the utility level; (ii) increase end use efficiency; (iii) promote locally available resources not currently being used, such as rainwater harvesting; (iv) promote substitution of resource use, e.g. use of waterless sanitation; and (v) use economic instruments to bring about an improvement in resource usage, such as use of tariffs. In order for any IUWRM strategy to work, there is need for full participation by all stakeholders, including staff of relevant organizations and community members (UNEP-International Environmental Technology Centre, 2003).

This paper describes how a partnership of various stakeholders in Zaragoza, Spain has enhanced a water-saving culture in the city. This analysis was carried out as part of an integrated research project funded by the European Union (EU), whose overall objective is to apply IUWRM concepts for achievement of effective and sustainable urban water schemes in the 'city of tomorrow (i.e. projected 30-50 years from now)'. The five-year SWITCH (Sustainable Water management Improves Tomorrow's City Health) project aims at developing efficient and interactive urban water systems and services in the city's geographical and ecological setting, which are robust, flexible and responsive to the many pressures of global change. Zaragoza is one of the partner cities for the SWITCH project, and is a demonstration city for the research activities under the (DM) work package of the project. The objective of the DM work package is to develop and test holistic DM tools, encompassing social, commercial and physical aspects, in order to reduce water wastage and provide educational materials for the benefit of service providers.

Background on the City of Zaragoza, the study setting

The city of Zaragoza, situated in the central area of the River Ebro basin, is the capital of Aragón region in North-eastern Spain. Zaragoza, with a mean elevation of 199m above seal level, experiences a hybrid of continental/Mediterranean climates, characterized by long winters (about 121 days with temperatures lower than 10°) and long summers (about 150 days with temperatures higher than 17°). Zaragoza is situated in a semi-arid region with an average annual precipitation of 314 mm, and a potential evapotranspiration rate of 795 mm per year (Arbués and Villanúa, 2006; Arbués, et al, 2004). To mitigate against the widely varying seasonal flow rates of River Ebro, 138 dams have been constructed on the river since the 1930s, providing a total storage capacity of 687,300 m^3 (Penagos, 2007).

The 2001 national census put the population of Zaragoza at 614,905 (a 31% increase with respect to the 1970 population), making it the fifth largest city in Spain (Arbués and Villanúa, 2006). While 96% of the city population currently live in the central cores dominated by high buildings (of between 6-12 floors), the suburban areas with single-family homes have shown a higher growth rate, in line with an increase in real disposable income (Arbués and Villanúa, 2006). As a result, the average household occupancy rate has reduced from 3.04 to 2.72 people per household between 1991 and 2001 (Arbués et al, 2004). The increasing income levels over the past couple of decades have invariably led to higher affluence, which has in turn resulted in higher household water consumption rates.

Water and sewerage services to the city residents are provided by Zaragoza City Council, through centralized municipal departments. Raw water for the city supply is abstracted from the River Ebro, mainly through the Aragón Imperial Canal. Although there are plentiful groundwater resources in Zaragoza, underground water has not been exploited for the municipal water supply, mainly because it contains high concentrations of minerals such as sulphates, nitrates, sodium and magnesium (Arbués et al, 2004). To respond to the increasing water demand, the city council has in the past focused on supply-side options, namely abstracting surface water further away from Zaragoza, through construction of dams, barrages, aqueducts and canals, the development of the Yesa dam being the most recent such project (Arbués and Villanúa, 2006). This paper demonstrates how Zaragoza City Council is turning round to implement some aspects of IUWRM to respond to the growing water supply needs.

Methods

The main objective of this study was to find out how various stakeholders in the City of Zaragoza have been engaged to enhance a water-saving culture in the city, mainly through behavioural changes and use of water saving devices/equipment. This study was conducted in 2007 as an early part of a larger five-year SWITCH research project, and provides a snapshot of what has already been done by stakeholders in Zaragoza on the front of DM. The main methods of data collection were (i) review of departmental reports, grey and published literature; (ii) key informant interviews; and (iii) non-participant observations. In Zaragoza City Council, key stakeholders that were interviewed represented the Environmental Education Section of the Local Agenda Department, Infrastructure Department, Pricing Unit and Department of Public Health. Others were key informants from the Department of Economics, Zaragoza University and Fundación Ecología y Desarrollo (FED), the environmental NGO that spearheaded the project.

Findings and discussion

The launch of the first phase of 'Zaragoza: The Water-saving City' Project

There was a serious drought in Spain during the period 1991 to 1995, which prompted Zaragoza City Council, the water service provider in Zaragoza to impose a variety of water restrictions. Consumers were unhappy about the restrictions, as evidenced by numerous public demonstrations. Furthermore, there were disagreements and confrontations between various regions of Spain about mass transfer of water through building dams, tunnels and channels. A survey carried out in 1997 showed that about 60% of the respondents could not remember or were ignorant of water saving strategies in the households (FED, 1998). This paradox stimulated Fundación Ecología y Desarrollo (FED), a Spanish environmental Non-Governmental Organization (NGO) to develop a pilot project focused on improving the efficiency of urban water use (Garrido et al, 2005). FED wanted to demonstrate that the water shortage problem could be solved using a cheaper, more environmentally friendly, and socially acceptable approach (FED, 1998).

FED developed the 'Zaragoza: Water Saving City' project in 1996, and opted for a phased approach to its implementation. Other founding partners included The European Union LIFE programme, Zaragoza City Council, Aragón Regional Government, Ibercaja (a national Spanish savings bank) and four other private companies (Balay, Jacob Delafon, Contazara and RST). With a budget of 0.87 million Euros variously contributed by the founding partners, the first phase of the project kicked off in February 1997, for two years, while the second phase ran from 2000 to 2002. The first phase, focusing on 'small steps, great solutions', sought to have a systematic focus on all aspects that individually and institutionally determine a water culture such as institutional policy framework, technology, knowledge/information, regulations and consumer habits. Based on the principle of shared responsibility, the intervention was also designed to create a collective challenge which would bring about participation of all stakeholders in the city, and build on the synergy of these partnerships to (i) create awareness of the need for water-saving; (ii) promote information about simple water-saving technologies; (iii) work towards creating a water-saving city, which would be set an example for the outside world; and (iv) save water without sacrificing comfort.

In concrete terms, the first phase aimed at saving at least 1,000 million litres of water in the homes of the city of Zaragoza per year (FED, 1998). For this objective to be achieved, there was need to promote the following actions: (i) change of attitude towards water use and consumption, leading to behavioural change; (ii) provision of information, education, training and advisory services which assist consumers who wish to take action to reduce their water use; (iii) replacement of old equipment with new water-saving devices; (iv) acquisition of new water-saving sanitary fittings (e.g. flushing toilets, taps, showers) and household appliances (e.g. washing machines and dishwashers); (v) the introduction of individual household hot water meters; and (vi) other actions that would save water, such as timely repair of leaks in the premises, and recycling of domestic water.

Partnerships for the water-saving project

It was recognized right from the project inception that improving a water-saving culture was a collective challenge, and required the full participation of all stakeholders that contribute to the water culture. As part of the preparation stage, the project deliberately sought the participation of all stakeholders including consumers, plumbers, policy makers, manufacturers, retail outlets, businessmen, building companies, financial institutions and architects. The steering partners actively participated in promotion strategies as well as monitoring and evaluating the implementation of the project. It was also important to involve elements of the business sector linked with manufacture, sale, distribution and installation of water fittings and equipments. Educational institutions and other civil society organizations collaborated in disseminating the promotion messages to the general public. Finally, the project worked with individual households and owners/overseers of large non-domestic premises that consume high volumes of water. Table 2.1 in Chapter 2 shows a summary of actions carried out with the key partners of the project.

Many organizations in Zaragoza participated in the water saving project. By the end of the first phase of the project, over 150 organizations were actively involved in project activities, such as distribution of information. The active partners included public institutions, NGOs, private companies, trade unions, professional bodies, community-based organizations and business associations. About 90% of the media houses in Zaragoza fully participated in the project. Furthermore, over 140 wholesale and retail establishments selling products related to water consumption, accounting for about 65% of all the traders, collaborated in the campaign. From the educational sector, 474 teachers and about 70,000 pupils from 183 schools collaborated in the educational programme on water-saving culture (FED, 1998). Clearly, in the two years of the first phase of the project, FED, the leading project partner successfully mobilized partnerships for enhancing water-saving culture in Zaragoza.

The second phase of the project

The aim of the project was fulfilled to a great extent as shown by a survey carried out in 1999 to evaluate the outcome of the intervention, the results of which were compared with those from the baseline study. The number of people aware of the importance of water-saving measures improved from 40% to 72% of the respondents. As a result of the campaign, there was an increase in water saving habits and use of water-saving devices in the households, leading to an overall saving of 1.176 billion litres of water in Zaragoza City, equivalent to 5.6% of annual domestic consumption. However, this evaluation survey also showed that the water saved was more as a result of behavioural change than adoption of water saving technology (Edo & Soler, 2004; FED, 2001).

The project partners recognized that emphasis on only behavioural change will not make a sustainable impact in conservation of water: there was need to adopt an integrated strategy, including adoption of water-saving technology. As a result, the second phase of the project, entitled 'Zaragoza, water saving city – 50 good practices' was initiated to widen and extend the intervention to non-domestic sectors, and at the same time consolidate the achievements realized by emphasizing the use of water-saving technology in the households. This phase was implemented from June 1999 to March 2003, and aimed at developing 50 best practices for efficient water use in selected public buildings, industries, and parks/gardens, such that these demonstration centres become a reference and model for others in the respective sub-sectors (Edo & Soler, 2004; FED, 2001).

Proactive representatives of the sub-sectors of parks/gardens, public buildings (e.g. health centres, schools, offices), and industries participated. Through continuous promotion activities, other members of the sub-sectors were kept informed of the progress of these demonstrations and were encouraged to adopt the tested good practices. The Parks and Gardens Section of the City of Zaragoza was a key participant, and by extension committed several private firms managing 36 green zones in the city, covering about 2.4 million sq metres. Other institutions that took part in the study included educational institutions, health centres, hospitals, residences for the elderly, university halls of residence, hotels and sports centres. A few industries involved in the extraction and transformation of non-energetic minerals, metal transformation and manufacturing enterprises dealing with food, wood and plastic also participated in the project (Edo & Soler, 2004).

Initially, preliminary surveys were conducted in the participating organizations to map out existing consumption rates and current polices and practices on water use and conservation. Thereafter, detailed audits were undertaken to evaluate the installations and practices, and make recommendations for more efficient water use. The audits solicited data on (i) description of water consumption fittings; (ii) consumption rates and costs; (iii) maintenance costs; and (iv) the environmental situation (i.e. the policy and level of sensitization, mapped through a staff survey). The auditors also developed a plan of action to improved the efficiency of water use, and supported the organization in the implementation process. Other organizations and companies in the sub-sector were kept informed of the progress, and were encouraged to participate in the project (Edo & Soler, 2004; FED, 2001).

By the end of the phase, 30 good practices were achieved in efficient water use in buildings for public use. Typical examples were (i) a shopping mall that achieved 92% water savings through a change in floor cleaning methods; (ii) an educational centre that saved 70% through environmental education; and (iii) a car-washing company that saved 75% through water re-use (Edo & Soler, 2004). Similarly, 13 good examples were established in the parks/gardens sub-sector, mainly through careful consideration of the design of the lawns, selection of the plant species, and water methods (*ibid*). In industries, huge savings were made in at least 9 enterprises through modification of the production and cooling processes, ranging from water recycling, water recirculation and reverse osmosis (*ibid*). The performing organizations were recognized by awards of certificates of proficiency, and were also recognized in various media and in national, regional and international forums. Furthermore, practical guidelines for efficient water use in the non-domestic sector were published and widely circulated. These publications include practical eco-audit guidelines for hotels, offices, industries, hospitals and educational institutions; and practical guidelines for dry-land gardening (Iglesias and Moneo, 2005).

Similarly, audits were also carried out in selected households, with the aim of promoting water-saving technology. As a result, a practical handbook on efficient water use in the homes was produced, which provided guidelines for householders to evaluate their water consumption rates, and adopt good practices for water use efficiency by installing technological devices and changing their habits. Households were offered subsidized kits of household water-saving devices, such as shower heads, tap devices and double-flush cisterns. The activities involving use of water-saving technology were carried out in full collaboration with the enterprises concerned with manufacturing, distribution and/or installation of the water-saving devices. Technical staff from these firms were continuously sensitized, kept informed of the project activities, and their profiles were widely circulated to the consumers.

The overall outcome of both phases of the project 'Zaragoza: the water-saving city' have been quite significant. Average water consumption in the households of Zaragoza reduced from 107 litres per capita per day in 1996 to 99 litres per capita per day in 1999 (Iglesias and Moneo, 2005). These figures are well corroborated with operational data for Zaragoza City Council, which show that, with an increase in population of 6.3% between 1996 and 2004, water supplied to the city reduced by 14% during the same period (Zaragoza City Council, 2006). To consolidate these achievements, another phase was launched in November 2006. 'Zaragaza, a water saving city: 100,000 commitments' aims to solicit for commitments from individual consumers for achieving efficient use of water in their premises.

Conclusion

The results of the initial fieldwork for the SWITCH research project in Zaragoza, as reported in this paper have been highly dependent on secondary data. It is hoped that as the research process progresses, primary data will be obtained, which will lead to improved validity and reliability. Notwithstanding these limitations, there is enough evidence to show that the first two phases of the project 'Zaragoza, a water saving city' have largely achieved their objectives. The success of this project, which was initiated and championed by Fundación Ecología y Desarrollo (FED), an environmental NGO, shows that although it is important for the state to provide a facilitating role for successful public action, non-state organizations with able and dedicated leadership can successfully spearhead and coordinate public action. The success of this project also demonstrates that partnerships, awareness-building and technology can be combined to achieve a substantial increase in water use efficiency. It is however important that all stakeholders are involved in the process right from the inception of the project. It is also important to acknowledge that there are many innovative people out there in the general population 'lying low' with their untapped capacities. These potential skills need to be mobilized and mapped to various roles and functions for overall achievement of the project objectives.

Another key lesson learnt from the success of this project is the need for phasing the implementation, and ensuring that there are specific time-bound targets for each phase. Since environmental projects require the participation of many stakeholders, including actions at individual households, a phasing approach is more likely to sustain the motivation of a myriad of participants. The successful implementation of this project has enabled Zaragoza to be categorized as a model city for efficient water use. It is no wonder, therefore, that this project was selected as one of the 100 most successful interventions for sustainable urban management by the UN-HABITAT. The methods used in this project could easily be adapted to other urban areas for more efficient urban water management.

Acknowledgements

The authors would like to thank all the stakeholders in Zaragoza City that provided various documents and took part in this study. The study was carried out as part of the activities under the EU-funded SWITCH Project.

References

Arbués, F. and Villanúa, I. (2006) Potential for pricing policies in water resource management: estimation of urban residential water demand in Zaragoza, Spain, *Urban Studies*, 43(13), 2421-2442.

Arbués, F.; Barberán, R. and Villanúa, I. (2004) Price impact on urban residential water demand: a dynamic panel data approach, *Water Resources Research*, 40(11), W11402, doi:10.1029/2004WR003092.

Edo, V.V. and Soler, M.F. (2004) Saragossa, 50 examples of efficient water use in the city, Water Science and Technology: *Water Supply*, 4(3), 111-122.

Fundación Ecología y Desarrollo (1998) *Zaragoza, saving water city (Spain)*, available at http://habitat.aq.upm.es/bpes/onu98/bp439.en.html [accessed on 9 August 2007].

Fundación Ecología y Desarrollo (2001) *Zaragoza, saving water city – 50 best practices*, unpublished report, Zaragoza, Spain.

Iglesias A. and Moneo, A (eds (2005)), *Drought preparedness and mitigation in the Mediterranean: Analysis of the organizations and institutions*, Options Méditerranéennes: Série B. Etudes et recherches, n.51, Zaragoza, Spain.

Penagos, G. (2007) *Systems analysis of Zaragoza urban water system (Spain): A preliminary assessment of environmental sustainability*, unpublished MSc dissertation, UNESCO-IHE Institute for Water Education, Delft, The Netherlands.

Savenije, H. and van der Zaag, P. (2002) Water as an economic good and demand management: paradigms with pitfalls. *Water International*, 27(1), 98-104.

UNEP-International Environmental Technology Centre (IETC), (2003) *Integrated Urban Resources Management Strategy: Water*, UNEP, Nairobi.

UN-HABITAT (2004) *State of the world's cities*, 2004/05, UN-HABITAT, Nairobi, Kenya.

UN-HABITAT (2006) *State of the world's cities*, 2006/7, UN-HABITAT, Nairobi, Kenya.

UNITED NATIONS (2007) *The Millennium Development Goals Report 2007*, UN, New York.

White, S.B. and Fane, S.A. (2001) Designing Cost Effective Water Demand Management Programs in Australia, *Water Science and Technology.* 46,(6-7),.225-232.

Zaragoza City Council (2006) *Management and use of water in Zaragoza,* unpublished departmental report, Zaragoza, Spain.

8

Use of multiple economic instruments for water demand management: case study of Zaragoza, Spain

Sam Kayaga

Introduction

Effective water demand management programmes involve the water service provider taking a holistic approach that considers a combination of measures and instruments with a potential for water conservation in a given context. Measures are the specific activities that need to be carried out in order to achieve a reduction in water use. The service provider uses various instruments to ensure that the chosen measures are put in place or taken up by the end users (Turner et al, 2006). There are three main categories of instruments available to a service provider: communicative, regulatory and economic.

Communicative instruments involve public education and use of marketing tools to change users' behaviour and invoke water efficiency consciousness. Regulatory instruments are 'command-and-control' tools used by government authorities to establish requirements such as specifying standards to be met and technologies to be used for achieving these standards (Cantin, Shrubsole and Ait-Ouyahia, 2005). On the other hand, economic instruments are market-based instruments that aim to stimulate water users to voluntarily adopt water-efficient behaviours. This paper focuses on the economic instruments and provides a case study of how they have been used in combination with other measures to reduce water consumption in the City of Zaragoza, Spain.

What are economic instruments?

Economic instruments (EIs) have been interchangeably referred to as market-based instruments in some literature. The use of EIs gained prominence in the 1970s when polluter-pays principles were first advocated. EIs may be defined as '...the use of market-based signals to motivate desired types of decision-making. They either provide financial rewards for desired behaviour or impose costs for undesirable behaviour' (Cantin, Shrubsole and Ait-Ouyahia, 2005, p.2). The overall aim of EIs is to shift the costs of resource use or pollution control from society to end users. Use of EIs in the field of environmental management aims at modifying the behaviour and decisions of stakeholders and individuals for the promotion of environmental protection, encouraging optimal rates of resource use /depletion, and for providing financial resources to support environmentally-friendly practices (Mattheiβ et al, 2009).

There are two broad categories of EIs: those that use existing markets and modify the market prices of goods and services such that existing environmental impacts are considered by the users; and those that create new markets for environmental goods and services. Examples of instruments that operate within existing markets are application of tariffs for existing services; levying of environmental taxes and charges on the degradation/pollution and/or extraction of natural resources; and provision of financial incentives and/or subsidies for good environmental practice. On the other hand, new markets for environmental goods and services could be created, which would function by either confronting directly the demand and supply of environmental good and services, or using intermediary structures to cause this confrontation. Table 8.1 provides further description and examples for each type of instrument.

Overall, EIs are considered more efficient than command-and-control approaches, encourage continuous improvement programmes, and stimulate development of innovative technologies (Cantin, Shrubsole and Ait-Ouyahia, 2005). However, for EIs to deliver results the following aspects should be considered:

- Given the existence of a variety of EIs, with each one having multiple variations, it might be worthwhile developing criteria for selecting the most promising instrument for the operating environment.

- It is necessary to carry out a situational analysis and if need be implement pilot case studies to identify which combination of EIs will be most cost-effective.

Table 8.1. Main economic instruments for the water sector (Adapted from Mattheiβ et al, 2009 and Cantin, Shrubsole and Ait-Ouyahia, 2005)		
Type of Instrument		Function(s)/main purpose(s)	Examples

Type of Instrument		Function(s)/main purpose(s)	Examples
Taxes and charges	Water tariffs	To collect financial resources for the functioning of a given water service. To promote efficiency in water use	Tariff for drinking water & sewerage services Tariffs for irrigation water
	Environmental tax	To collect financial resources for the central budget for offsetting negative environmental impacts. To influence behaviour	Tax on pollution discharge or water abstraction Tax on polluting input (e.g. pesticide)
	Environmental charge	To collect financial resources that are allocated to support environmentally friendly practices & projects To influence behaviour	Charge on pollution discharge or water abstraction Charge on polluting input (e.g. pesticide)
Subsidies	Subsidies on products	To increase attractiveness of 'green' products and production factors that have limited negative environmental impact	Subsidies for biological agricultural products
	Subsidies on practices	To promote the application of practices and production processes that limit negative impacts on water resources or produce positive environmental externalities	Subsidies for water saving devices
Markets for environmental goods/services	Tradable permit for pollution	To ensure an optimum allocation of pollution among sectors	Market for pollution permits among polluters of a given river basin
	Tradable permit for abstraction	To ensure an optimum allocation of water quantity among sectors	Informal water markets in irrigation schemes
	Compensation mechanisms	To establish mechanisms where environmental degradation leads to financial payment that is allocated to alternative actions to compensate for the degradation	Compensation for ecological degradation in the aquatic ecosystem
Property rights		To promote responsible resource management	Ownership rights Use rights

- Application of new EI will most likely require changes in institutional and legal framework.

The most commonly used economic instrument for water demand management is the water tariff. Choosing an appropriate pricing strategy is difficult. Ideally the tariff should be based on full-cost pricing, to include all costs of construction (including opportunity cost of capital), operating, maintaining and replacing the infrastructure, as well as externality costs such as environmental degradation. However, not only is it difficult and challenging to take into account all the externalities (Cantin, Shrubsole and Ait-Ouyahia, 2005), in many cases policy makers are reluctant to recover full costs from consumers. The next sections discuss in more detail the use of tariffs as an economic instrument for water demand management.

Using tariffs as an economic instrument for water demand management

The use of water tariffs as economic instruments for managing water demand is made possible through application of the universal economic theory of supply and demand to water supply services. For goods in a perfect market, prices guide the choice of how much to produce and how much to consume, and serve to balance supply and demand. These conditions do not fully apply to water services: studies have shown that water consumption is not substantially affected by changes in price, especially in the short term. Water services are price elastic, i.e. changes in price induce relatively smaller changes in consumption. The main reasons behind the price inelasticity of water services are (Chesnutt et al, 1997):

- drinking water services have no perfect substitutes to which the consumer can resort. The situation is different for other water usages which have limited substitutes;

- water utility bills are usually an insignificant proportion of household expenditures;

- for many consumers water tariffs have been quite low, and consumers have not developed the incentive for monitoring and changing water use patterns in response to price changes;

- water bills are usually combined with other utility bills such as wastewater, gas, electricity etc., which makes it difficult to discern the changes in water prices; and

- historically, changes in water prices have most likely been less than the change of rate of inflation.

In spite of these unique characteristics, water services also conform to the law of supply and demand; the only difference is that the demand supply curve may not depict the profile that is typical for other goods and services. Changes in demand when the price for water changes may be difficult to observe, especially when water tariffs are low, and long-term response to price changes may overshadow short-term response. Previous studies have shown that water services have greater potential for long-term responsiveness, such as investing in more water efficient fixture and landscaping (Chesnutt et al, 1997). However, demand responsiveness to the price of water is difficult to figure out, since the price of water in the future will most likely increase due to several factors, such as escalating costs for replacement of ageing infrastructure and/or capital costs for expansion, and adherence to more stringent service quality standards.

Most water service providers use historical costs as the basis for computing water prices. Historical costs are those incurred by the service provider in provision of services. Tariffs based on historical costs signal to the consumers the past cost consequences of usage decisions, and give an impression that resources used for future investments to provide water services will cost the same as those used in the past, which in most situations is not the case. Use of historical costs may not send the right cost signals for encouraging water conservation. A tariff structure is said to be conservation-oriented if it encourages efficient water use and discourages wastage of the water resource. These two conditions can only be fulfilled if the customers' water bills communicate the full cost of providing water services, including the cost of exploiting new water supplies. These tariffs should be based on marginal cost pricing and resource efficiency goals (Chesnutt et al, 1997).

Marginal-cost pricing reflects the reality that the cost of developing new water resources will most certainly be higher than historical costs. Marginal costing reflects estimates of the costs of developing the next increment of supply required to satisfy a given increase in water demand. The challenge is how to estimate marginal costs where cost accounting capacity is low. One of the most widely used methods that approximates to marginal cost pricing is the average incremental costing (AIC) method. The accuracy of marginal cost pricing could be improved as cost accounting methods improve, future cost methods are better defined, and as the use of marginal cost pricing is embraced by more service providers (Chesnutt et al, 1997).

Designing a water tariff structure can be a complex process, depending on the multiplicity of objectives the service provider aims to achieve. Tariffs could be utilized as economic tools to improve the efficiency of water resource allocation between different users, and promote efficient water use. However, pricing could also aim to achieve objectives of equity, public health, environmental efficiency, financial stability, public acceptability, and transparency (Arbués, Garcia-Vilinas and Martinez-Espineira, 2003). These objectives are often difficult to combine. Barberán and Arbués (2009) state that the most commonly used criteria for domestic water rates design are full cost recovery, efficiency, equity and simplicity.

The most commonly used tariff structure that approximates to a conservation-oriented rate is the increasing block tariff. Not all increasing block tariffs are water conserving, as the unit price charged fforego the last unit of water consumed may not be equal to the marginal cost of new water supplies. In most cases, increasing block tariffs are designed to fulfil the objective of equity or fairness rather than efficient water use. However, if the community members are fully involved, it is possible to design a tariff structure that achieves both equity and efficiency goals. On the other hand, the main goal of many service providers is the collection of sufficient revenue to cover administrative, operating and capital costs. Conservation-oriented tariffs promote variable charges at the expense of fixed rates, and this induces a level of revenue volatility in cost recovery. Revenue for service providers with ineffective/inadequate meter reading, bill compilation and bill delivery would be more negatively affected by a proportionately larger variable component of the tariff. However, the uncertainty surrounding future revenue streams for the utility can crop up with most water tariff structures, and service managers have a variety of strategies at their disposal for coping with it.

The benefits of using a conservation-oriented tariff structure may be classified as short- and long-term. In the short term, conservation will reduce operating costs associated with treating and pumping, or even purchase of bulk water from wholesale suppliers, where applicable. On the part of the consumer, conservation will reduce water and energy bills. A major benefit of water conservation in the long run for the service provider, consumers and society as a whole is the postponement of additional source development and water treatment capacity. The application of conservation-oriented water rates by service providers experiencing demand growth helps to extend the useful service life of the infrastructure, and also signals the actual cost of system expansion to the users and policy makers. Conservation-oriented rates could also lead to better allocative efficiency for service providers who have disparity in service levels between high- and low-income consumers (Kayaga & Motoma, 2009). The rest of the paper describes how the water utility in Zaragoza, Spain has made advances in enhancing water demand management in the city, by redesigning the water tariff structure, and providing subsidies on products and practices for water demand management.

Using a combination of economic instruments: The case of Zaragoza, Spain

Background information on Zaragoza

The city of Zaragoza is the capital of Aragon region, one of the 17 autonomous communities of Spain. Aragon borders to the North with France, and the Pyrenees separates both territories. Zaragoza is situated on the central stretch of the Ebro Valley, which crosses the Northeast of Spain, and is mid-way on the stretch of Madrid to Barcelona, 300 kilometres from either of the cities. The municipality of Zaragoza has a surface area of 967 km2 and a population of 682,283 inhabitants (2008), which accounts for about half of Aragon's population (AYTO, 2009). The economy of Zaragoza is supported by commercial and industrial activity. The commercial activity in Zaragoza is composed of numerous shopping centres. Industrial activity is diversified, but mainly dominated by light metal and car auxiliary industries such as Opel.

Zaragoza, with a mean elevation of 199m above sea level, experiences a hybrid of continental/Mediterranean climates, characterised by long winters (about 121 days with temperatures lower than 10°) and long summers (about 150 days with mean temperatures higher than 17°). Zaragoza is situated in a semi-arid region with an average annual precipitation of 314 mm, and a potential evapotranspiration rate of 795 mm per year (Arbués and Villanúa, 2006; Arbués, et al, 2004). The main source for the city's water supply is the River Ebro, the biggest Spanish River, with an average volume of flow of 400 m³/second. To mitigate against the widely varying seasonal flow rates of River Ebro, 138 dams have been constructed on the river since the 1930s, providing a total storage capacity of 687,300 m³ (Penagos, 2007).

Water and sewerage services to the city residents are provided by Zaragoza City Council, through centralized municipal departments. Although there are plentiful groundwater resources in Zaragoza, underground water has not been exploited for the municipal water supply, mainly because it contains high concentrations of minerals such as sulphates, nitrates, sodium and magnesium (Arbués et al, 2004). To respond to the increasing water demand, the city council has until the 1990s focused on supply-side options, namely abstracting surface water further away from Zaragoza, through construction of dams, barrages, aqueducts and canals (Arbués and Villanúa, 2006). The Canal Imperial of Aragon, which receives its water from the River Ebro 80 km north of Zaragoza is the city's water supplier. The water from the Canal is considered as a protected river bed and waste spill is forbidden, therefore the quality of Zaragoza water is higher than that of the Ebro. Both the quality and quantity of water is expected to improve with the completion and commissioning of the construction of the Yesa Reservoir by the end of 2010 (Benadi, E, 2008).

Raw water from the Ebro River flows by gravity to Casablanca water treatment plant (with a capacity of $6m^3/sec$), where it is treated using conventional treatment processes of screening, oxidation of organic matter using sodium hypochlorite, flocculation/coagulation using aluminium sulphate, sand filtration and disinfection with sodium hypochlorite. The water treatment plant also incorporates a sludge treatment plant (using activated carbon), that contributes to environmental sustainability objectives. Potable water is stored in reservoirs (with storage capacity of 180,000 m^3) located at the same site, before it is distributed to the consumers through more than 1,100 kilometres' length of a reticulation network. The network is mainly composed of pipes made of the following materials: (i) asbestos cement (34%); (ii) ductile iron (48%); (iii) reinforced concrete (6.5%) and (iv) µPVC (5.5%).

All functions relating to the urban water cycle in Zaragoza are managed by various departments of AYTO, the City Council of Zaragoza, as follows:

- Raw water abstraction, treatment and distribution of drinking water are the responsibility of the Infrastructure Department.

- Installation, operation and maintenance of the water distribution system is provided by the Infrastructure Department, and/or by private sector companies, under the supervision of the Department.

- Municipal wastewater is collected through a sewerage network, to wastewater treatment plants owned by AYTO but managed by private sector firms. This is a combined sewerage network which also collects storm water as well as partially treated industrial wastewater and delivers them for treatment and eventual disposal back to the River Ebro.

The Municipal Institute of Public Health of the City of Zaragoza manages quality assurance procedures for both water supply and wastewater treatment systems. There are two wastewater treatment plants in Zaragoza: Cartuja, with a design treatment capacity of 259,200 m³/day and Almozara (design capacity of 34,560 m³/day) treating 85% and 15% of the City's wastewater flows, respectively. The first three treatment processes are primary decantation, activated sludge and secondary decantation. Thereafter, the processes at Cartuja involves phosphorous removal, while at Almozara, the effluent is disinfected. Sludge is treated at both plants and heat is recovered and transformed into electricity at Cartuja, while biogas is recovered for energy production at Almozara.

Reforming the tariff to make it more demand-responsive and equitable

Prior to 2007, the water tariffs set by Zaragoza City Council, the service provider, were mainly driven by financial and political considerations, rather than economic considerations. Each applicant paid a one-off connection fee at the time of joining the water supply network. Comprising a fixed fee and a volumetric-based rate, the tariff structure was more aligned to collecting enough revenues to cater for a politically acceptable part of the costs of providing water services (Arbués and Villanúa, 2006). The monthly fixed fee was based on the street category where the building was located, and mainly depended on the length/width of the street, and whether there were any commercial enterprises. Not enough quantitative data were collected to determine these rates, and therefore, the criteria did not have much correlation with the socio-economic status of the household. There were instances where the rates were allocated mainly based on political criteria (Barberán, and Arbués, 2009).

Table 8.2. Zaragoza official tariff rate: fixed charges in Euros per month (rates for 1996-1998 converted from Spanish Pesetas at the 2002 exchange rate of 1€ to 166.4 Pesetas)

	Street categories			
	Special	First	Second	Third
1996-1998	3.48	2.85	2.40	2.13
2002	3.85	3.15	2.65	2.35

Source: Arbués and Villanúa (2006) and Barberán and Arbués (2009)

129

Table 8.2 shows the fixed part of the tariff in the mid-1990s and 2002. The Table shows that the rates remained constant between 1996 and 1998, and were adjusted by up to 10% between 1998 and 2002, which are minimal changes in real terms. For the general tariff, the volumetric charge was computed on an incremental basis with 134 steps based on average pricing. A single price was charged for each unit of water consumed, which increased progressively as the daily consumption of a household went up.

Arbues & Villanua (2006) computed the marginal price (i.e. the price of an extra unit of water) using the following formula quoted from Griffin, Martin and Wade (1981):

$$\text{mgprice} = \frac{\Delta\,(\text{avgprice} \times q)}{\Delta\,q}$$

In the formula, *mgprice* is the marginal price, *avgprice* is the average price, and q is the change in water consumed. In all cases the average cost was lower than the marginal cost, the latter plotting into a typical increasing block tariff made up of four blocks (Barberán and Arbués, 2009). The price levels for the first block were low enough, to enable universal access to the basic lifeline supply for basic physiological household use. The price levels increased progressively in the progressive blocks. Table 8.3 shows a simplified structure of the marginal costs for the year 2002.

Table 8.3. Zaragoza official tariff rate: simplified volume-based rates of marginal prices in 2002 (Lucea, 2010)		
Category	Consumption Block (m³/month)	Marginal price (€ per m³)
Category 1	0 - 6	0.21
Category 2	6 - 13	0.45
Category 3	13 - 35	1.13
Category 4	Over 35	1.58

Zaragoza City Council also operated a special tariff structure to cater for large families and low-income households. 'Large families' were defined as families with more than five members (two parents and three or more children) or four or three people if one of the children is physically/mentally disabled. Large families received a 25% subsidy on their bills, as long as their monthly consumption did not exceed 30 m³. Low-income households were defined as those families whose total income was less than 1.1 times the minimum official wage and who owned no property, financial or other assets (except their dwelling place) worth over 3.5 times the annual minimum wage. The subsidy for low-income families was 90% of the variable charge if consumption was less than 10 m³/month, 75% if monthly consumption is 10-35m³, plus 50% of the fixed charges. These subsidies were difficult to administer and transaction costs were high.

Zaragoza City Council initiated a long-term programme to reform the tariff in 1995, in which changes were implemented in a step-wise fashion. The overall aim of the change programme was to design a tariff structure that achieved the following key objectives (Lucea, 2010):

- adequate revenues: The price levels should be high enough to ensure recovery of operation and maintenance costs; capital costs; and opportunity cost of capital. The ideal situation is to move towards recovery of full accounting model for the whole water cycle, which also includes opportunity cost of the water resource and environmental costs.

- social equity: The allocation of costs among consumers in the same category should be based on the principle of obtained benefits. Consumers receiving the same benefits should pay the same costs (horizontal equity) and those with different benefits should pay different costs (vertical equity). Furthermore, uses of water for health and hygiene should be differentiated from water used for value addition such as for commercial/industrial activities.

- universal access to the basic water service: The tariff structure should ensure that all households have access to basic 'lifeline' consumption at an affordable price. There should be subsidies targeted at vulnerable households.

- efficiency: The tariff structure should encourage efficient use of the water resource by the consumers. The unit price of water should approximate to a marginal cost.

- simplicity and transparency: The tariff structure should be simple to administer on the part of the service provider, and easily understood by the customer.

- economical: application of the tariff should generate the lowest cost to the service provider and the customer. The administrative procedures should provide maximum efficiency for both the service provider and the customer.

As part of the programme, research was carried out by the University of Zaragoza to provide an empirical basis for the tariff reform. The first part of the study (1996-2002) used bi-monthly billing information and data on socio-economic characteristics of over 1500 households to estimate a regression model of water price, climate, household income and household size. The model was used to estimate elasticity of demand with respect to price, household income and household size. The second part of study (2002-2004) used data from 9000 randomly sampled households to analyse their 2002 water prices and came up with concrete recommendations for the design of the tariff structure based on the normative criteria of full cost recovery, efficiency, equity and simplicity.

The key findings of the study by the University of Zaragoza were that price, household size, and household income were all significantly related to water demand. However, the average price elasticity of demand η_{av} was -0.08, classified as price-inelastic, which means that an increase in price produces a disproportionately lower reduction in water consumption. On the other hand the household income and household size displayed higher elasticity to demand, at averages of 0.79 and 0.48, respectively (Arbués and Villanúa, 2006). Other key findings were that every household required an average basic minimum amount of 3.5 m^3 per month to maintain the common good in the home, while each resident required an additional 2.5 m^3 of water per month, which decreased with household size, along economies of scale.

The low price elasticity of demand for water services in Zaragoza may be explained by the following factors (*ibid*):

- many of the household uses of water fulfil basic physiological needs such as drinking, cooking, personal hygiene and household cleaning. Water for these requirements is highly inelastic, as customers do not have good substitutes;

- drinking water services are provided by a legal monopoly, giving no choice to consumers to change suppliers;

- water services bills constitute a negligible portion of the household income (about .5% of average household income), thereby providing no incentive for customers to change to more efficient water faucets and devices; and

- the tariff structure based on average prices gives a wrong impression to customers that each additional unit of consumed water is paid at a progressively lower rate.

A major observation from the University of Zaragoza study was that the existing variable water tariff structure composed of 134 steps of average price levels, coupled with the generally low price levels could not send clear signals to consumers to use water more efficiently. Furthermore, price subsidies for large families and those with disabled children considered the household as a unit, rather than targeting members of the household, which meant that the subsidies did not fully serve their purpose, as they were more of a tax redistribution tool than for social equity (Lucea, 2010). The study recommended that price levels should be increased and the volume-based tariff structure should be rationalized, not only to enable customers have a closer representation of the real marginal cost, but also to make it simpler to understand.

As a result of the reforms informed by the University of Zaragoza study, the fixed tariff since 2007 has been made proportional to the diameter of the service pipeline. About 90% of the household connections are serviced by meters of diameter sizes ranging between 13-20mm, with consumptions up to 300 m^3 per property per month. Households on a 20mm diameter service pipe pay standing charges of €2.30 and €1.50 per month for water and wastewater services respectively, equivalent to a total of €3.80 per household per month (Shirley-Smith et al, 2008). In 2009, fixed charges contributed 47.4% of all revenues obtained from households compared to 16% for non-domestic consumption (Lucea, 2010). Larger volume domestic users pay a higher proportion of their bills through the variable rates. For instance, the fixed proportion of the water bills for consumers with service meter connections of over 30mm diameter was notably lower, at 35.1% (*ibid*).

Important reforms were made to the variable component of the water rates, alongside increasing the percentage of properties fitted with consumption meters. By the end of 2008, over 330,000 properties had service meters, giving a metering percentage of 99.8% (Lucea, 2010). Price levels were significantly raised to bring them closer to full financial cost recovery. For instance, price levels were increased by 30% between 2004 and 2005 (Shirley-Smith et al, 2008). Further increments were made in the subsequent years, and by 2009, over 95% of the full costs at the historical cost model were covered by the tariff (Lucea, 2010). Furthermore, the increasing block tariff was redesigned to cater for per capita water consumption, with only three increasing blocks, which combines the objectives of enhancing equity among various social groups, simplifying the tariff structure, and applying disincentives for water wastage.

To minimize technical difficulties and management costs of keeping updated information of household size, the first two blocks are based on household use (general tariff), while the last block caters for per capita consumption, differentiated for households with bigger families whose standard consumption is higher than the volume established for the first two blocks of the general tariff. The price for the last block is twice the price of the second block, as a disincentive for water wastage, and cover extra administrative charges for applying the per capita water tariff. Six is the set minimum size of the household for which the optional per capita tariff may be offered. Table 8.4 shows a sample tariff structure for six people, based on the findings of the research that 3.5m³ is normally used for the 'common good' in the household, while each person in the household will need 2.5 m³ per month. Only 97 households applied for the per capita tariff in 2008. These were categorized as follows: seven members of the household – 62; eight members – 24; nine members – seven; 10 members – one; and 11 members – three numbers.

Table 8.4. The 2009 Zaragoza variable water tariff, based on a family size of six (Lucea, 2010)	Rates based on water consumed (€/m³)		
	Water	Sewerage	Total
Block 1: Fixed consumption (3.5 m³per HH) plus 1 person's 2.5 m³ per month = 6 m³ for one occupant in a month	0.162	0.171	0.333
Block 2: Fixed consumption (3.5 m³ per HH) plus up to 6 person's consumption at 2.5 m³ per person per month, i.e. over 6 m³ and up to 18.5 m³ per HH per month	0.389	0.41	0.799
Block 3: Consumption over 18.5 m³ per HH per month	0.778	0.821	1.599

Incentives for water conservation

Other than disincentives for wastage of water, Zaragoza Municipal Council also offered economic incentives to households that reduced their consumption rates. These economic instruments may be classified as price subsidies to promote good environmental practices (Mattheiβ et al, 2009; Cantin, Shrubsole and Ait-Ouyahia, 2005). Starting in 2002, households that reduced their consumption by at least 40% during the financial year were entitled to a 10% discount on the bill. In subsequent years, they were expected to reduce consumption by at least 10% per annum in order for them to benefit from a similar price rebate. Table 8.5 shows the number of households that made water savings, and benefited from the economic incentives between 2002 and 2006.

Table 8.5. Number of households benefiting from the economic incentives for water saving (Lucea, 2007)					
Start Year	Households with new commitments	Further subsequent savings of at least 10% in the Year			
		2003	2004	2005	2006
2002	1,708	375	66	2	1
2003	27,741		5,331	487	123
2004	24,331			2,956	721
2005	27,929				4,635
2006	33,274				

The table shows that some households had the capacity to continuously make savings in subsequent years. For instance, of the 1,708 households that reduced their consumption by 40% in 2002, 375 of these made a further 10% reduction in 2003. A further 10% savings were achieved by 66 households in 2004, two households in 2005 and one household in 2006, respectively. As can be seen from column 2 of the table, the scheme was being embraced by an increasing number of households, which contributed to overall reduction in water consumption in Zaragoza.

'Zaragoza, the water saving city' programme

The economic instruments described above complemented activities carried out as part of a long-term programme implemented by a partnership of key stakeholder organizations in Zaragoza that aimed at improving the efficiency of urban water use in Zaragoza, as described in Chapter 7. This programme was implemented between 1997 and 2008, and was coordinated by Fundación Ecología y Desarrollo (FED), a Spanish environmental Non-Governmental Organization (NGO), who deliberately engaged active participation of all key stakeholders such as consumers, educational institutions, plumbers, policy makers, manufacturers, retail outlets, entrepreneurs, building companies, financial institutions and architects (Kayaga et al, 2008). The programme was structured into four phases (Fundación Ecología y Desarrollo, 2010), which were described in greater details in Chapter 7:

- Phase 1: 'Small steps, big solutions', aimed at making changes on all aspects that individually and collectively affect the water using culture in homes, public buildings, large consumers and the general public.

- Phase 2: '50 good practices' focused at reducing water consumption of large consumers of water such as public buildings, industries, parks and gardens.

- Phase 3; 'School for efficient water use', whose objective was to extend the good practices resulting from the first two phases, and for Zaragoza to become a role model city for efficient water use.

- Phase 4: '100,000 Zaragoza commitments', whose objective was to collect, verify and document 100,000 public commitments for efficient water use, and showcase Zaragoza as a 'World Water Capital City' at the EXPO 2008 international exhibition on water and sustainable development.

This programme succeeded in engaging all key stakeholders in the city to create awareness of the need for water-saving, promoted information about simple water-saving technologies, and inculcated a water-saving culture among the residents of the city of Zaragoza. When the project was initiated the overall objective was to reduce Zaragoza's domestic water consumption from 84.8 million m^3 per year in 1997 to less than 65 million m^3 by 2010, factoring in the increase in city's population. This target was achieved at an earlier date of 2006, as shown in Figure 8.1. The figure shows that although the city's population increased from 606,069 in 1997 to 682,283 by 2008 (an increase of over 12%), the city's overall water consumption reduced from 84.8 to 61.5 million m^3, respectively, which was a reduction in consumption of 27% (AYTO, 2009).

This programme used a combination of measures and instruments to cause behavioural changes among the end users and encouraged them to make structural changes in their fixtures and appliances, which resulted in the positive changes in water use efficiency. An evaluation survey conducted at the beginning of the second phase of the water-saving programme showed that water conservation was more as a result of behavioural change than adoption of water-efficient devices (Edo & Soler, 2004). The most visible measures were educating the end users to promote their consciousness for water use efficiency so that they could change their behaviour. There is no doubt, however, that the economic instruments discussed in the bulk of this paper contributed to the behavioural change, as can be extrapolated from data shown in Table 8.5.

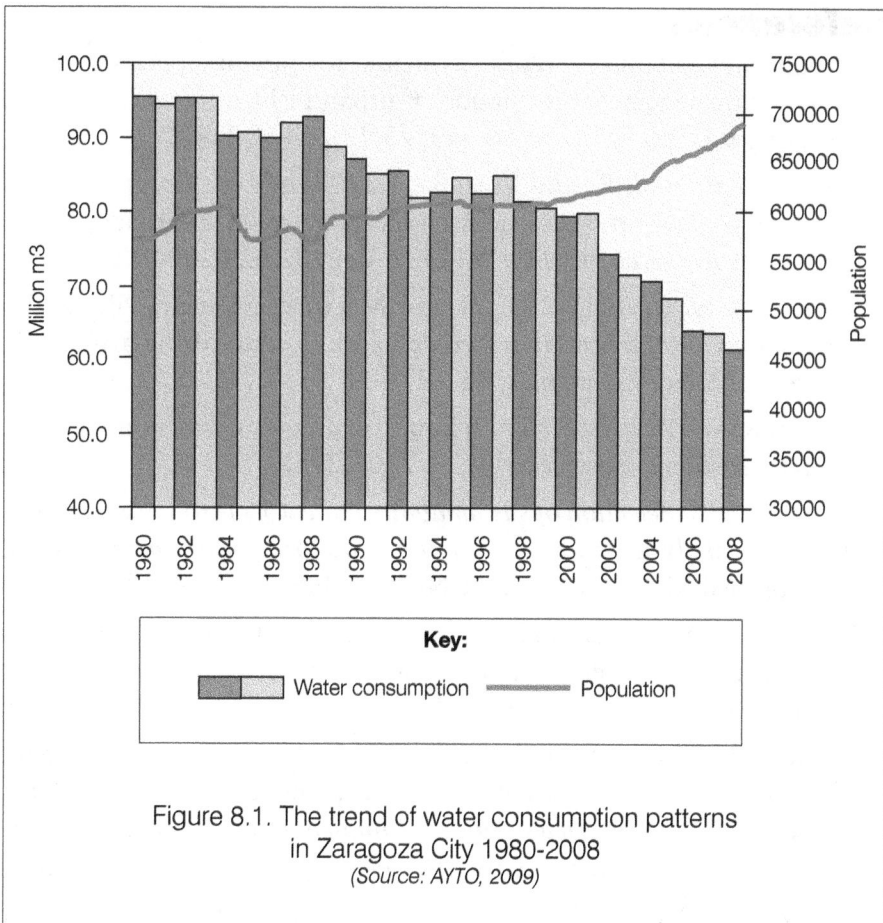

Figure 8.1. The trend of water consumption patterns
in Zaragoza City 1980-2008
(Source: AYTO, 2009)

Concluding remarks

This case study shows how a combination of economic instruments has been used to effectively contribute to an integrated programme for water demand management in Zaragoza. The effectiveness of tariffs and other economic instruments for water demand management depends on optimally aligning them with the socio-economic status of the consumers. There are two key lessons from the Zaragoza case study for other cities. Firstly, economic instruments will make a significant contribution to water conservation only if implemented in combination with other water demand management measures. Secondly, there is need to carry out research in order to accurately map the socio-economic status of the consumers so as to design effective economic instruments.

137

References

Arbués, F. and Villanúa, I. (2006) Potential for pricing policies in water resource management: estimation of urban residential water demand in Zaragoza, Spain, *Urban Studies*, 43(13), 2421-2442.

Arbués, F.; Barberán, R. and Villanúa, I. (2004) Price impact on urban residential water demand: a dynamic panel data approach, *Water Resources Research*, 40(11), W11402, doi:10.1029/2004WR003092.

Arbués, F., Garcia-Vilinas, M. A. and Martinez-Espineira, R. (2003) Estimation of residential water demand: a state-of-the-art-review, *Journal of Socio-Economics*, 32,.81-102.

Barberán, R. and Arbués, F. (2009) Equity in domestic water rates design, *Water Resources Management*, 23, 2101-2118.

Benadi, E. (2010) *Selection of sustainability indicators through an iterative life cycle analysis procedure for the Zaragoza urban water system*, unpublished MSc dissertation, UNESCO-IHE, The Netherlands.

Cantin, B.; Shrubsole, D. and Ait-Ouyahia, M. (2005) Using economic instruments for water demand management: introduction, *Canadian Water Resources Journal*, 30(1), 1-10.

Chesnutt T.W.; Beecher, J.A.; Mann, P.C.; Michael Hanemann, W.; Raftelis, G.A.; McSpadden, C.N.; Pekelney, D.M.; Christianson, J. and Krop, R. (1997) *Designing, evaluating and implementing conservation rate structures*, The California Urban Water Conservation Council, USA.

Edo, V.V. and Soler, M.F. (2004) Saragossa, 50 examples of efficient water use in the city, Water Science and Technology. *Water Supply*, 4(3), 111-122.

Fundación Ecología y Desarrollo (n.d) *Design and implementation of awareness programmes*, available at http://www.ecodes.org, [accessed on 6 September 2010].

Griffin, A.H.; Martin, W.E. and Wade, J.C. (1981) Urban residential demand for water in the United states: comment, *Land Economics*, 55(3), 252-256.

Kayaga, S. and Motoma, R. (2009) Using tariffs as a demand management instrument: the case of Kampala, in: *Proceedings of the 34th WEDC International Conference, Addis Ababa, Ethiopia*, May 2009. WEDC, Loughborough University, UK.

Kayaga, S.M.; Sainctavit, L.; Smout, I.K. and Bueno, V. (2008) Partnerships for enhancing the water-saving culture in Zaragoza, Spain, in: *IWA World Water Congress, Vienna, September 2008*.

Lucea, J.G. (2010) *Criteria used to design the water tariff*, unpublished internal document, AYTO, Zaragoza, Spain.

Mattheiβ, V.; Le Mat, O. and Strosser P. (2009) *Which role for economic instruments for the management of water resources in Europe?* In search of innovative ideas for application in the Netherlands, Report for the Dutch Ministry of Transport, Public Works and Water Management.

Penagos, G. (2007) *Systems analysis of Zaragoza urban water system (Spain): A preliminary assessment of environmental sustainability*, unpublished MSc dissertation, UNESCO-IHE Institute for Water Education, Delft, The Netherlands.

Shirley-Smith C., Cheeseman, C. and Butler, D. (2008) Sustainability of water management in Zaragoza city, *Water and Environmental Journal*, 22(4), .287-296.

Turner, A., Willets, J., Fane, S., Giurco, D.; Kazaglis, A. and White, S (2006) *Planning our future urban resources – A guide to demand management in the context of Integrated Resource Planning*, Institute for Sustainable Futures, University of Technology, Sydney.

Zaragoza Ayuntamiento (AYTO) (2009) *Zaragoza in SWITCH Project*, unpublished report, Zaragoza, Spain.

9

Using a tariff structure for water demand management in cities of developing countries: the case of Kampala, Uganda

Sam Kayaga

Need for integrated water resources management

While the population in many industrialized countries is either decreasing or constant, the population in most developing countries is increasing rapidly, resulting in an overall global population increase. The current global population is estimated to be 6.9 billion people, of which 82% live in developing countries (UN-HABITAT, 2009). Consequently, per capita water availability is steadily declining. The water scarcity situation is compounded by the major impacts of climate change on the water resources, and the practical distribution problems concerned with time, space and affordability, leading to a widening gap between demand and supply in many parts of the world.

The water scarcity situation will escalate in the urban areas of less developed regions where it is estimated that the urban population will increase from about 2.57 billion in 2010 to 3.95 billion in 2030, accounting for 94% of the global urban population in the period 2010-2030 (*ibid*). The situation calls for the adoption of integrated water resources management (IWRM). IWRM is an approach that '...promotes the coordinated development and management of water, land and related resources, in order to maximize the resultant economic and social welfare in an equitable manner without compromising the sustainability of vital ecosystems' (Global Water Partnership, 2006, p.22). The principal components of IWRM in urban areas are supply optimization; demand management; participatory

141

approaches to ensure equitable distribution; improved policy, regulatory and institutional framework; and intersectoral approach to decision-making (UNEP-International Environmental Technology Centre, 2003). Water demand management (WDM), one of the components, may be defined as the development and implementation of strategies, policies and measures aimed at influencing demand, so as to achieve efficient and sustainable use of the scarce water resource (Savenije and van der Zaag, 2002).

WDM contrasts with the conventional supply-driven approach to water resources management, whose response to the ever increasing water demand is development of new water sources. There are five major categories of WDM measures (White and Fane, 2001): those measures that (i) increase system efficiency at the utility level; (ii) increase end use efficiency; (iii) promote locally available resources not currently being used, such as rainwater harvesting; (iv) promote substitution of resource use, e.g. use of waterless sanitation; and (v) use economic instruments to bring about an improvement in resource usage, such as use of tariffs. The remainder of this paper describes the application of tariffs for WDM in the city of the future. The next section provides an overview of how tariffs could be designed as a tool for water demand management. Thereafter follows a description of a case study that was done on how the existing water tariff structure for the City of Kampala, Uganda could be redesigned to be more water-conserving.

Water tariffs as a WDM instrument: an overview

Water pricing is intrinsically related to sustainable urban water management. A water tariff that effectively contributes to sustainable urban water management will aim to achieve a balance among multiple complex goals. Several authors such as Beecher & Shanaghan (1999), Chalvatzi et al (2007) and Barberán & Arbués (2009) emphasize five key goals i.e. efficiency, optimality, equity, viability and simplicity. A water tariff should promote overall efficiency for society, in terms of sending the right signal that leads consumers to consume, and producers to produce, an appropriate amount of the good or service, and will promote efficient water usage. Ideally, water prices should reflect the incremental cost of producing an additional unit of a good/service, i.e. should be based on marginal cost pricing. Optimality aims at having the efficient prices also reflecting least-cost capital investment, operation and maintenance of the infrastructure services. Equity objectives take into account socio-economic aspects, especially ability to pay for the services and ensure that low-income and other vulnerable groups of society gain access to services. Viability objectives ensure that the price recovers at least the financial costs of water services, so as to enable revenue sufficiency and financial stability of the service provider. Finally, simplicity of the tariff structure is to ensure that not only do the consumers understand its provisions; it should be simple enough for the employees of the service provider to explain it, defend its rationale, and enforce it.

Designing a water tariff structure can be a complex process, depending on the multiplicity of objectives the service provider aims to achieve. A tariff that maximizes on the objective of inducing water efficiency will be an instrument for water demand management. In order to fully understand the role of tariffs in water demand management, it is useful to internalize the price elasticity of demand properties of various levels of water usage. Price elasticity of demand (Ed) may be defined as the ratio of the percentage change in quantity demanded to the percentage change in price (Case and Fair, 1989). Since the relationship between the price and the quantity demanded is usually negative, Ed is also negative, but its absolute value is usually quoted in the literature. When the change in quantity demanded is higher compared to the price change, demand for that good or service is said to be elastic, i.e. less than one. On the other hand, if changes in price induce relatively small changes in consumption, economists label that demand as price inelastic.

Water used for basic household requirements such as drinking, cooking, washing utensils and sanitation/personal hygiene has been observed to be price inelastic, mainly because potable water has no close substitutes to which consumers can switch. Water for other purposes has limited substitutes, and is more price elastic. Therefore, while applying general demand-supply economic laws to water services, it is important to identify the different elasticity properties applying to various end uses, and obtain averages over the range (Chesnutt et al, 1997). Price elasticity of demand depends on various socio-economic factors such as the proportion of household income, composition of the household members and level of awareness of the benefits of water services. It also depends on availability and relative cost of alternative water services, and timeframe in which price changes have been effected. Therefore, price elasticity of demand varies from one community to another, and over time, depending on the changes in these conditions.

Price elasticity of demand studies are quite elaborate, and, although many service providers design their tariffs with the objective of achieving full cost recovery, very few tariffs are designed to be water-conserving, which would require price elasticity and other socio-economic data. Tariffs of most water service providers aim at (a) recovering the financial costs of service delivery; (b) allocating costs to water users(s) in an equitable manner, i.e. according to costs that they actually incur; (c) taking into account socio-economic factors, ensuring equity of access and protecting low-income households; and (d) fostering transparency in cost estimation and allocation of subsidies and cross-subsidies (Chalvatzi, Manoli and Assimacopoulos, 2007).

Service providers may fix their tariff based on either historical costs or marginal costs. Historical costs represent the costs actually incurred by a utility in providing the service, and such costs signal to consumers the past cost consequences of usage decisions. On the other hand, prices based on incremental or marginal costs provide signals to consumers about future cost consequences of their usage decisions, and reflect an estimate of the costs of developing the next increment of supply required to satisfy additional demand. Economists generally consider marginal cost pricing to provide better price signals in terms of achieving efficiency in supplying and using the water resources (Chesnutt et al, 1997). Such price signals provide a basis for consumers to make informed decisions about how to use water efficiently. Although conservation rates generally have higher price levels, in real terms they may lower customer bills: if water prices are set to reflect the higher cost of new supply, customers have the incentive to use less water, total system demand would grow less quickly, and the need for more costly system expansion would be deferred.

In designing a tariff structure, the first decision to be made is whether all costs will be recovered from the water service rates. Some service providers may have the option of alternative sources of funding such as through general national taxes, although design of conservation rates necessarily requires full cost recovery. Secondly, should the tariff structure be differentiated across various customer classes? Examples of customer groups are residential, commercial and industrial; according to size of service pipeline; and for households, based on the service levels such as house connection, yard tap or public standpipe. Thirdly, should the tariff have fixed and variable components? All revenues could be recovered through variable charges, or fixed charges could cover metering, billing and other administration charges; the fixed charges could be varied for different customer classes. Fourthly, should the structure cater for seasonal changes in consumption? If so, how should the peak period be defined?

Fifthly, should the rates vary by block of water usage or should they be uniform for all customers or those within a class? If so, what would be the number of blocks, how would they be decided, and what would be the unit rates for each block? (Chesnutt et al,1997).

It is a challenge to make the afore-mentioned decisions for designing a conservation rate structure that also achieves the goals of equity, optimality, viability and simplicity. It would not be practical for the service provider to aim for a perfectly efficient tariff structure, but rather one that is as efficient as possible, given the trade-offs that need to be made to achieve other objectives. A key trade-off that is usually made by service providers is balancing the objectives of a conservation-oriented tariff - which is enhanced by a variable component (commodity or volumetric charges); and revenue stability – which is enhanced by a fixed component. Fixed charges may also be variously termed as customer charges, minimum charges, demand charges, connection fees or access fees. Fixed charges are designed to recover costs related to standard expenditure for maintenance and administration costs. Ideally, volumetric charges cover all other costs related to volumes of water used.

The most commonly used tariff structure that approximates a conservation-oriented rate is the increasing block tariff. Not all increasing block tariffs are water conserving, as the unit price charged to the last unit of water consumed may not be equal to the marginal cost of new water supplies. In most cases, increasing block tariffs are designed to fulfil the objectives of equity or fairness rather than efficient water use. However, if relevant socio-economic data are appropriately applied for the design of the structure, and the community members are fully involved, it is possible to design an increasing block tariff structure that simultaneously achieves efficiency, equity, viability, optimality and simplicity goals. Although not all consumers will be charged at marginal cost pricing, the increasing block tariff will allow service providers to charge efficient prices to more consumers than would otherwise be possible. However, there is a danger that the equity objective is negated by low-income consumers, normally falling in the lowest price bracket, who may on-sell water services to the un-served, thereby raising the periodic consumption to the higher price blocks (Boland and Whittington, 2003). This anomaly may be minimized by designing a tariff structure that caters for differentiated and all-inclusive services for the benefit of all consumers, including the unconnected (Sansom et al, 2004).

Study setting, objectives and methodology

Kampala, with an estimated population of 1.45 million, is the capital city and industrial hub of Uganda, accounting for about 65% of the national economic activities (UN-HABITAT, 2009; Beller Consult, Mott MacDonald and M&E Associates, 2004). About 45% of the city residents live in low-income informal settlements, with limited infrastructural public services (Beller Consult, Mott MacDonald and M&E Associates, 2004). The water and sewerage services in Kampala and 21 other major urban areas in the country are provided by the National Water and Sewerage Corporation (NWSC), a corporatized public-owned utility, and currently managed under the public law. The water treatment capacity for NWSC in Kampala was boosted in 2007 from about 120,000 to 200,000m^3/day, through commissioning of Gaba III water treatment plant, and, as of June 2007, it provided water services to 71% of the city's population, through 106,522 service connections (NWSC, 2007). According to the 2006-2009 NWSC corporate plan, challenges related to water resources affecting the achievement of NWSC's mission 'to provide efficient and cost –effective water and sewerage services…', are (NWSC, 2006):

- low water treatment capacity compounded by escalating water demand, as the city population increases;

- receding lake levels, with water levels in recent times being the lowest in past 40 years; and

- deterioration of raw water quality, as the lake shores are heavily polluted by human settlements and industrial activities.

Table 9.1. Tariff structure for NWSC water services between 2004 and 2008

Consumer category	Price (Uganda Shillings*/m^3)			
	2004/05	2005/06	2006/07	2007/08
Public standpipe	521	568	688	784
Domestic	806	879	1,064	1,213
Institutions / Government	993	1,082	1,310	1,493
Commercial <500m3/^{m}	1,379	1,462	1,716	1,931
Commercial 500 – 1500m3/^{m}	1,421	1,462	1,716	1,931
Commercial >1500m3/^{m}	1,324	1,324	1,496	1,601
Average commercial price	1,373	1,432	1,643	1,410
Overall average price	964	1,037	1,332	1,332

*about 1850 Uganda Shillings = 1 US$ at the time of the study.

Source: NWSC, 2006; 2007

NWSC is a semi-autonomous (state-owned) organization, which has previously wholly relied on public funding for capital investment costs. Since the management reforms in the late 1980s, the financial objective of NWSC has been to recover operation, maintenance and depreciation costs through tariffs; and use internally generated revenue for partial investment funding. As a result, the tariff structure has evolved over time, and the current tariff has a built-in indexation formula applied on an annual basis, to protect it from being eroded by inflation. The tariff structure at the time of the study was differentiated in increasing blocks according to the type of connection (i.e. public standpipe, household connection, institutional/government, commercial/industrial) with further block structures for industrial/commercial connections. Table 9.1 shows how the NWSC tariff structure has been adjusted between 2004 and 2008.

The objective of this study was to demonstrate how demand-responsive tariffs could be used as an economic instrument to encourage existing consumers to conserve water, and hence reduce the pressure placed on the infrastructure and the water resources in a developing country city such as Kampala. This study was conducted by developing a simple Microsoft Excel-based model using primary billing data for Kampala water supply area for one financial year (i.e. July 2006 to June 2007). 70,851 Monthly billing data sets for 70,851 households were received from NWSC in the form of a Microsoft Access database. These data were converted into an SPSS data set, and then examined to eliminate data corresponding to inactive accounts (i.e. disconnected from service either due to non-payment or technical faults during the study period), properties with incomplete entries, and entries with negative/zero consumption and/or billings. The remaining data translated to 54,024 household properties, arranged in a hierarchical order based on the customer reference numbers. Using SPSS, a five percent random sample was drawn, giving a total of 2,701 household properties.

Studies on price elasticity of demand are quite rare in developing countries, and no such studies have been documented with respect to Kampala. Since price elasticity of demand is an important input into a model for pricing decisions, a literature search was conducted to identify a city with similar socio-cultural-economic characteristics where price/demand studies had been conducted. The closest match for the parallel surveying method was the City of Cape Town, whose price elasticity estimated figures were reported in a study by Jansen og and Shulz (2006). The objective of the South African-based study was to provide greater understanding of the factors that influence water consumption, and provide an estimate for the price elasticity of demand of households living in Cape Town. Longitudinal data of monthly water consumption for 275 households were collected from July 1998 to June 2003, (i.e. a series of 60 observed readings per household). To make a panel data set, the water consumption data were combined with average monthly rainfall, mean temperature for this period, as well as household socio-economic data obtained through a questionnaire administered in July-August 2003. The major findings of the Cape Town study were that the price elasticity of demand ranged between -0.23 for low-, -0.32 for middle- and -0.99 for high-income households (Jansen og & Schulz, 2006).

The current study adopted socio-economic data from various studies conducted in Kampala. The key variables were:

- Average household size of five, as per the Uganda National Household Survey 2005/2006 (Uganda Bureau of Statistics, 2006);

- Average per capita water consumption estimates for three income categories (high, medium and low) obtained from a consultancy study by Beller Consult and Associates (2004).

- Estimated (2004) income ranges for customers of NWSC in Kampala, obtained from a DFID-funded study on water service connection charges and costs (Kayaga and Franceys, 2007) and adjusted by Uganda's national economic growth rate of 6% at the time.

Table 9.2 shows socio-economic data obtained from these studies, which were matched with the price elasticity of demand figures obtained by parallel surveying with Cape Town, and used as inputs into the pricing model.

Table 9.2. Model inputs derived from recent studies in Kampala and Cape Town

Income category	Data from Kampala studies			Est. Average Price Elasticity of Demand (Data from Cape Town)
	Estimated Income ('000 Uganda Shillings [UgX]*)	Average per capita consumption (litres)	Monthly Household consumption (m³)	
High income	> 1,403	144	> 22	0.99
Middle income	503 – 1,403	100	11 - 22	0.32
Low income	< 503	40	< 11	0.23

*about 1850 UgX = 1 US$ at the time of the study.

Sources: Uganda Bureau of Statistics, 2006; Beller Consult and Associates, 2004; Kayaga and Franceys, 2007; and Jansen og & Schulz, 2006

The following key assumptions were taken into consideration:

- the average household size is similar in all the income categories (i.e. 5 people per household);
- the lowest targeted level of service is a house connection – this could also be a secured yard tap;
- each household uses its own water service connection, with no sharing between the households;
- water consumed in the household is strongly correlated to monthly income;
- domestic water use patterns remain the same over the study period;
- annual price adjustments of 6% , indexed to inflation rates have negligible effect on demand for water;
- affordability to pay for water services conforms to the World Bank's rule of thumb of not more than 3% of the household income.; and
- the minimum water consumption in Uganda's urban areas is 30 litres per capita per day, which is 4.6 m³ per household per month.

The model was based on the following equation for Price Elasticity of Demand, Ed (Chesnutt et al, 1997):

$$Q_2 = \left[1 + \left(\frac{P_2}{P_1 - 1}\right) * E_d\right] * Q_1$$

Where

- Q1 is the initial quantity of water consumed, when the price is P1;
- Q2 is the adjusted quantity consumed when the price is changed to P2.

At the time of the study, NWSC charged a uniform rate of UgX 1,213 per cubic metre for all household consumption (i.e. P1 = 1,232 for all the three categories).

Figure 9.1 shows the data flow diagram for the model. All sampled households were allocated to the corresponding consumption blocks of low-, medium- and high consumption. They then were assigned with income levels. Next, the households were allocated price elasticity of demand, as per the results of the parallel survey with the Cape Town study. The lower limit of the income brackets for all the three categories were used as data inputs for the model. New prices were calculated for each consumption block, on the basis of affordability to pay of the households. Applying the price elasticity of demand function, the adjusted prices were then substituted to compute consumption rates for each sampled household. The model allocated households to final consumption blocks, depending on how the household responded to the price changes.

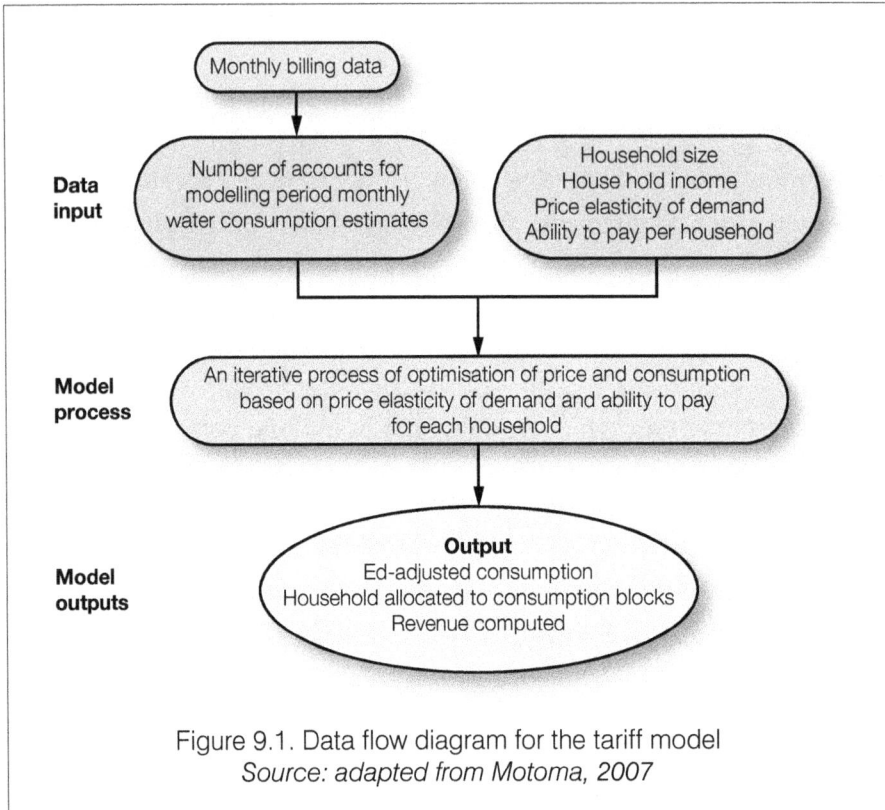

Figure 9.1. Data flow diagram for the tariff model
Source: adapted from Motoma, 2007

Results and discussion

Tariff structure

The model derived an optimal tariff which will not only conserve water, but will promote the equity objective based on the household affordability criteria. Figure 9.2 shows the current household tariff compared to the proposed tariff. It shows that in order to fulfil the equity criteria, the price for the first block (i.e. less than $11m^3$ per household per month) should be reduced by 2%. On the other hand the price for blocks 2 (11-$22m^3$ per household per month) and 3 (over $22m^3$ per household per month) should be increased by 13% and 58% respectively. These price increases would ensure that households pay no more than 3% of their household incomes. By charging these prices, the average volumetric charge for the household sector would increase by 8%.

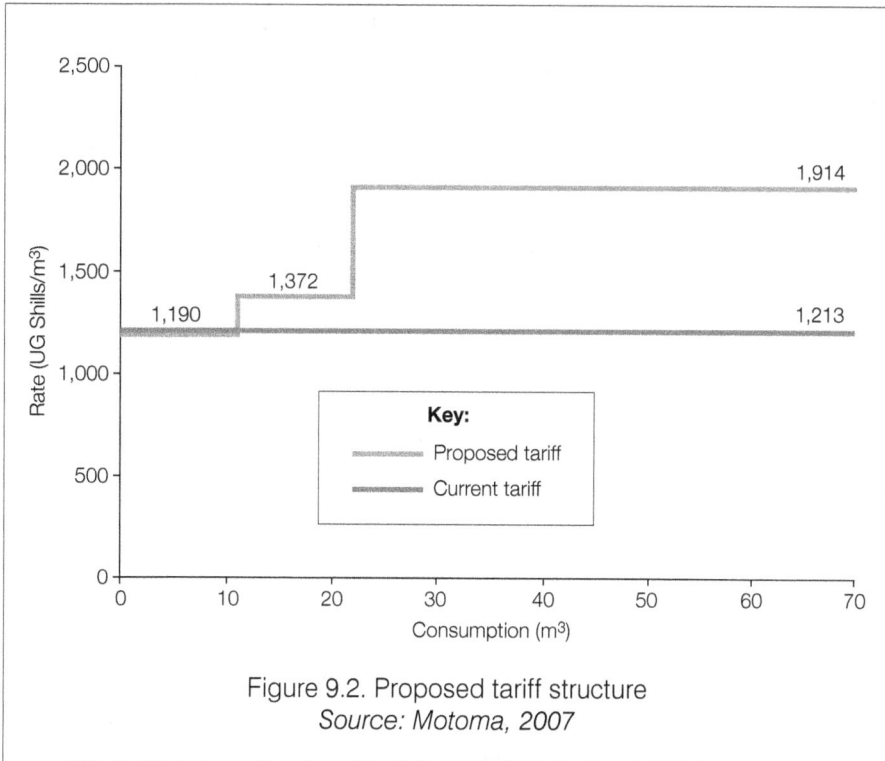

Figure 9.2. Proposed tariff structure
Source: Motoma, 2007

Water consumption

The key objective of enhancing water conservation will be achieved by the proposed tariff structure. The overall average per capita consumption for the household sector will change from 130 to 110 litres per capita per day, as shown in Figure 9.3. When disaggregated into consumption blocks, it can be seen that households falling into block 3 will be mostly affected by the new tariff structure, reducing their per capita consumption considerably. This is the consumption block where water savings will be realized There would be no change in per capita consumption for the first block, but a slight increase for the second block. The increase in the average per capita consumption in block 2 is mainly influenced by households previously in block 3, which will be forced to reduce their consumption and shift to the upper part of block 2 (i.e. closer to the upper limit of 22 m^3 per household per month), in response to the price change.

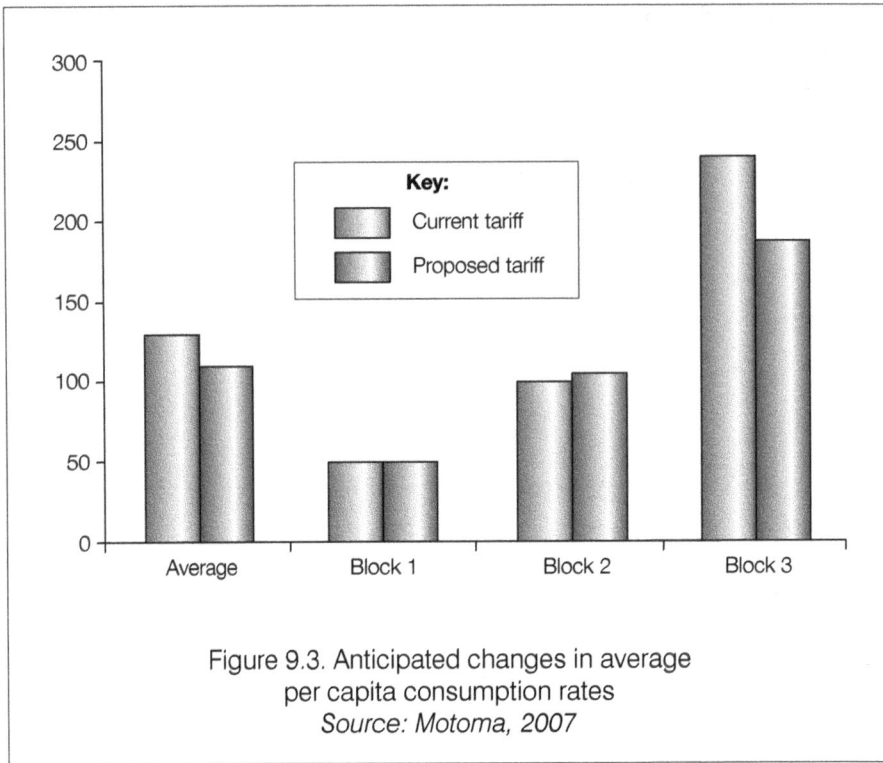

Figure 9.3. Anticipated changes in average
per capita consumption rates
Source: Motoma, 2007

Indeed, in the medium to long term period, many households are expected to adjust their consumption behaviours and patterns in response to the price change. The most affected category will be block 3, where it is anticipated that the proportion of household consumers will be reduced from 29% to 22%. All these consumers will revert to block 2, hence raising its share of consumers from 41% to 49%. On the other hand, since the price for block 1 has not significantly changed, we expect the share of consumers to remain constant at 29%.

The capacity of the new tariff to conserve water may be analysed by comparing the proportion of water consumed by the three blocks for the current and the proposed tariff structure, shown in Figures 9.4 and 9.5, respectively. The proportion of water consumed by the high income bracket would reduce tremendously from 55% (Figure 9.4) to 39% (Figure 9.5), while it would go up by 2% for block 1, and 15% for block 2. The proposed tariff structure therefore improves allocative efficiency, and its equity objective could be enhanced if the 'freed' water is redistributed to the un-served, who are usually living in low-income settlements of the cities of developing countries.

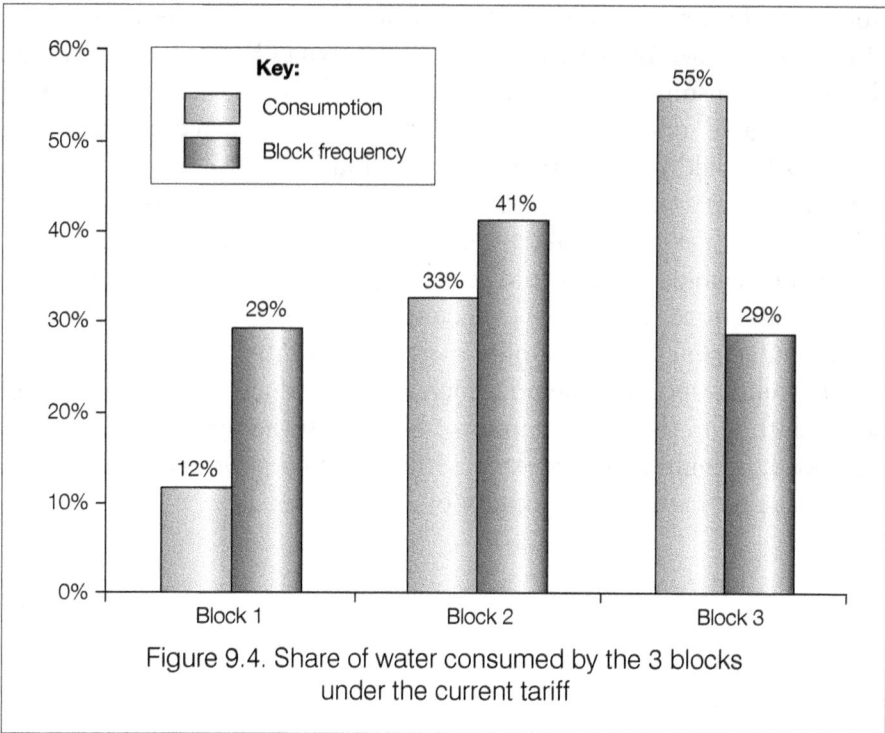

Figure 9.4. Share of water consumed by the 3 blocks
under the current tariff

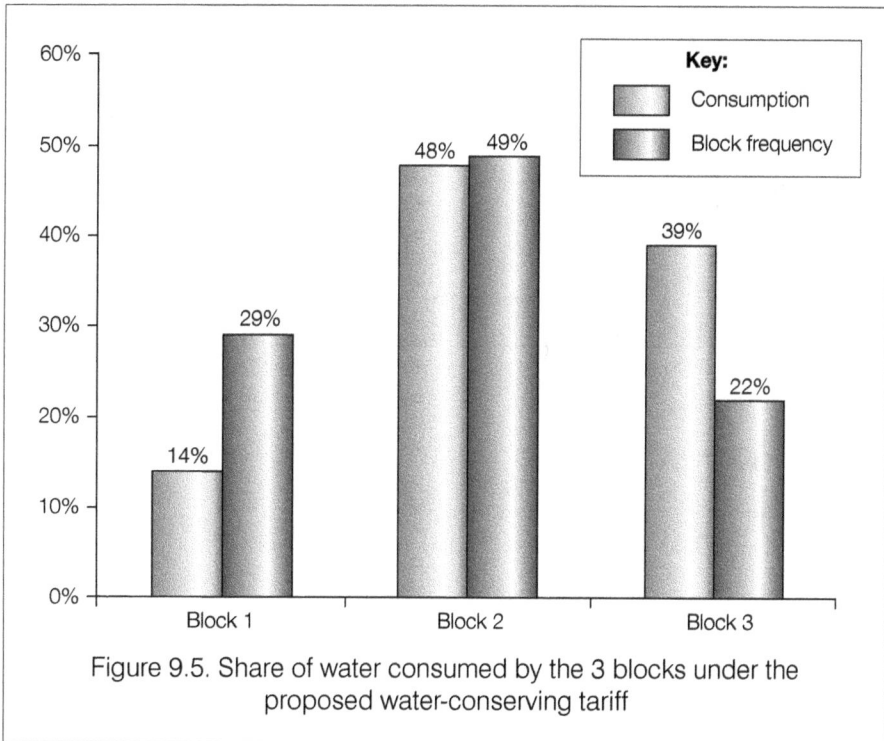

Figure 9.5. Share of water consumed by the 3 blocks under the
proposed water-conserving tariff

Adoption of a water-conserving tariff would lead to changes in the share of water consumed by the three blocks, as shown in Figure 9.6. The graph shows that consumers falling in block 1 would reduce their consumption by a negligible amount of 15,800m³ per year (0.8% reduction); those in block 2 would increase their consumption by 1,246,152 m³ per year (22% increase); but those in block 3 would reduce their consumption by 3,765,414 m³ per month (41% reduction). On the whole, consumption for the household sector would reduce by 2,535,074 m³ per year (15% overall reduction). The increase in consumption for block 2 is explained by the movement of households that are currently falling in block 3, which would respond to the price increase and reduce their consumption, hence shifting to the upper figures of block 2. If the water saving is well harnessed, it could serve an extra 230,460 urban poor people assuming an average per capita consumption of 30 litres per day.

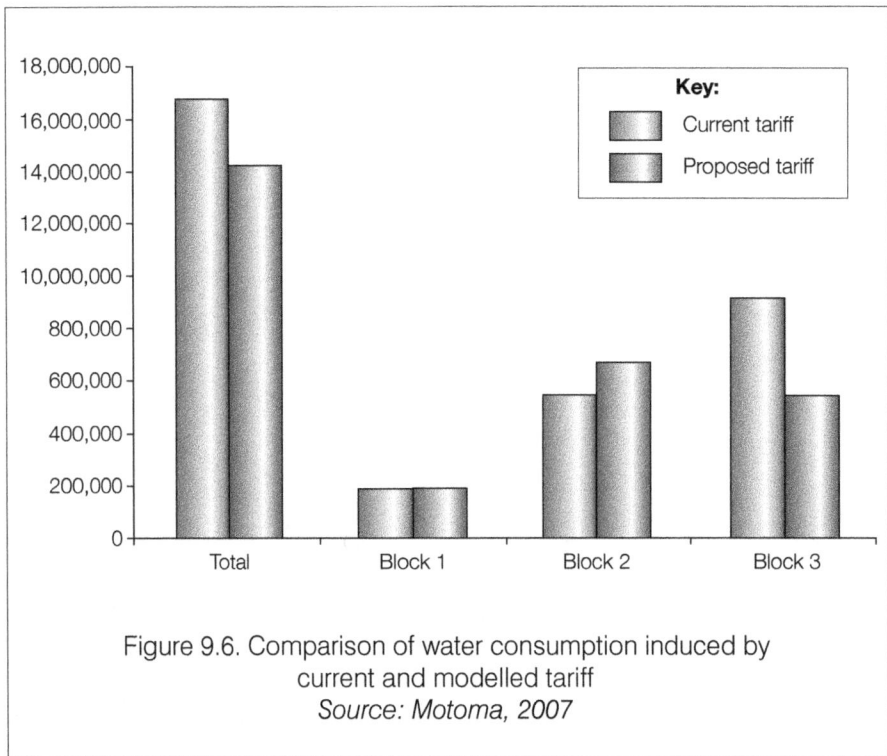

Figure 9.6. Comparison of water consumption induced by current and modelled tariff
Source: Motoma, 2007

Revenue collection

As discussed in Section 2, one of the key objectives of a tariff is its viability, i.e. to extent to which a tariff structure provides enough revenue stability to at least cover operation, maintenance and depreciation charges of providing the service. Assuming the 'freed' water is sold at the average price computed by the model, revenue collection would increase from UgX 20.328 billion to 22.035 billion, an increase of 8.3%, as shown in Figure 7. This result is in line with the economic principles which state that when demand is price-inelastic, price increases will lead to an increase in revenue; while price reduction will lead to loss in revenue. As can be seen all the consumption blocks have been assumed to have price elasticity of demand (Ed) less than 1 (i.e. inelastic). The water savings made could be utilized to expand services to low-income unplanned settlements in Kampala, where most households are not directly connected onto the city's water reticulation network, partly due to inadequate water in the supply system (NWSC, 2006).

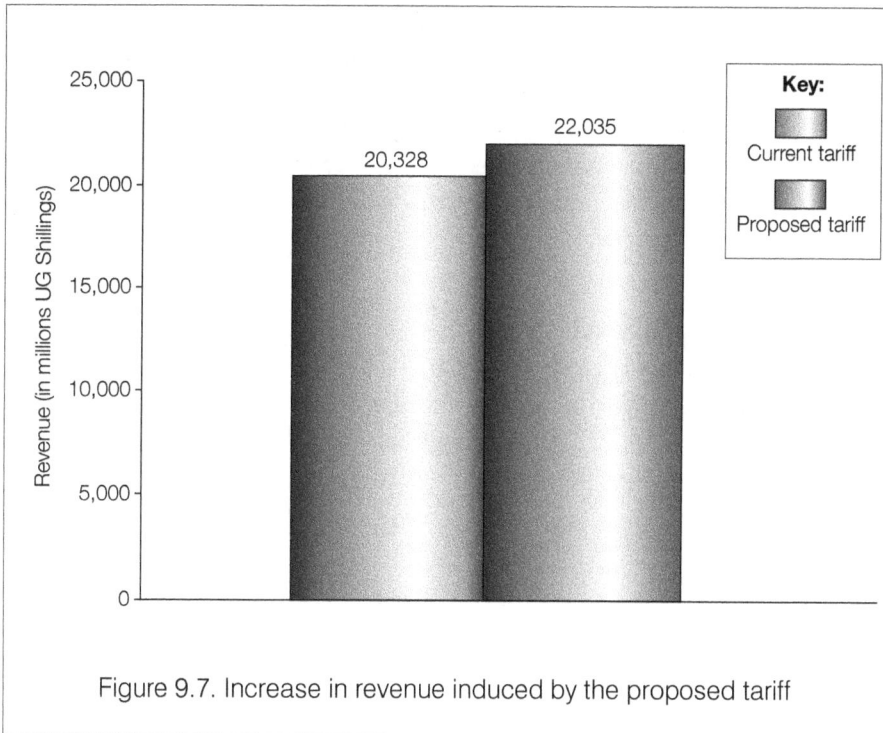

Figure 9.7. Increase in revenue induced by the proposed tariff

Conclusion

Adoption of integrated water resources management is necessary for coping with water scarcity brought about by an ever increasing global population, compounded by negative impacts of climate change. WDM is one of the key components of integrated urban water resources management. WDM could also be used in the short term to plug the supply-demand deficits currently existing in many cities of developing countries, and the use of water conserving tariffs is a WDM strategy that requires minimal investment. This paper reports on a case study conducted in Kampala on how water tariffs could be redesigned to not only conserve water, but also enhance social equity.

Through parallel surveying, the study adopted the price elasticity of demand for water of residents of Cape Town (South Africa), to develop a simple model for a water-conserving tariff for households in Kampala. The derived tariff can save 15% of water currently supplied to the household sector in Kampala, and low income households would find it more affordable to pay for a basic lifeline water requirement of at least 30 litres per capita per day. Furthermore, application of this tariff could increase the utility's revenues by 8%. Given an appropriate policy framework, the extra revenue generated could be invested to expand services to the un-served, who usually live in low-income settlements of the urban areas of developing countries. Water conservation tariffs have greater potential benefits in cities of developing countries where water services are usually excessively under-priced.

Acknowledgments

This case study was written based on an MSc dissertation by Mr Ramogodi Ishmael Motoma, MSc Student in 2006/07 at the Water, Engineering and Development Centre (WEDC), Loughborough University, UK. We are grateful for his permission to use it as a case study for the SWITCH Project.

References

Barberán, R. and Arbués, F. (2009) Equity in domestic water rates design, *Water Resources Management*, 23, 2101-2118.

Beecher, J.A. and, Shanaghan, P.E. (1999) Sustainable water pricing. *Water Resources Update* 114, 26–33.

Beller Consult and Associates (2004) *Sanitation Strategy and Master Plan for Kampala City*, Kampala.

Boland, J. and Whittington, D. (2003) The political economy of increasing block tariffs in developing countries, *Special Paper for Economy and Environment Programme for South East Asia.*

Case, K.E. and Fair, R.C. (1989) *Principles of Economics,* Prentice-Hall International: London.

Charvatzi, E., Manoli, E. and Assimacopoulos, D. (2007) Designing water pricing in the context of the Water Framework Directive (WFD) implementation: a case study in the river basis of Athemountas, Greece,in: *Proceedings of the 10th International Conference on Environmental Science and Technology,* Kos Island, Greece, 5-7 September 2007, pp. A196-A203.

Chesnutt T.W., Beecher, J.A., Mann, P.C., Michael Hanemann, W., Raftelis, G.A., McSpadden, C.N., Pekelney, D.M. Christianson, J. and Krop, R. (1997) *Designing, Evaluating and Implementing Conservation Rate Structures,* The California Urban Water Conservation Council, USA.

Global Water Partnership (2006) *Urban Water and Sanitation Services; An IWRM Approach,*(TAC Background Papers No.11), Stockholm, Sweden.

Jansen og A., and Schulz, C. (2006) *Water Demand Management and the Urban Poor: A study of the Factors Influencing Water Consumptions Among Households in Cape Town, South Africa,* (Working Series in Economics and Management, No 02/06), University of Tromso, Norway.

Kayaga, S. and Franceys, R. (2007) Costs of Urban Utility Water Connections: Excessive Burden to the Poor, *Utilities Policy,* 15(4), 270 – 277.

Motoma, R.I. (2007) *Modelling a Water Conserving Tariff for the City of Kampala,* Unpublished MSc Dissertation, Loughborough University.

National Water & Sewerage Corporation (NWSC) (2006) *Corporate Plan 2006-2009,* Kampala.

National Water & Sewerage Corporation (NWSC) (2007) *2006/2007 Annual Report,* Kampala.

Sansom, K., Kayaga S., Franceys, R., Njiru, C., Coates, S. and Chary, S. (2004) *Serving all urban consumers - a marketing approach to water services in low- and middle-income countries. Book 1: Guidance for government's enabling role,* WEDC, Loughborough University.

Savenije, H. and van der Zaag, P. (2002) Water as an economic good and demand management: paradigms with pitfalls, *Water International*, 27(1), 98-104.

The California Urban Water Conservation Council (2007) *Designing, Evaluating and Implementing Conservation Rate Structures*, California, USA.

Turner, A.; Willets, J., Fane, S., Guirco, D., Kazaglis, A. and White, S. (2006) *Planning our future urban water resources: A guide to demand management in the context of integrated resource planning*, Institute of Sustainable Futures, University of Technology, Sydney.

Uganda Bureau of Statistics (UBOS) (2006) *Uganda National Household Survey 2005/2006*, Kampala.

UN-HABITAT (2004) *State of the world's cities*, 2004/05, UN-HABITAT, Nairobi, Kenya.

UN-HABITAT (2009) *Planning sustainable cities: global report on human settlements*, UN-HABITAT, Nairobi, Kenya.

UNEP-International Environmental Technology Centre (IETC) (2003) *Integrated Urban Resources Management Strategy: Water*, UNEP, Nairobi.

United Nations (2007) *The Millennium Development Goals Report 2007*, UN, New York.

White, S.B. and Fane, S.A. (2001) Designing Cost Effective Water Demand Management Programs in Australia, *Water Science and Technology*, 46(6-7), 225-232.

Positive steps for management of non-revenue water in cities of developing countries: the case of Accra, Ghana

Sam Kayaga

Introduction

Water Demand Management (WDM) is a growing concept in the area of integrated urban water resources management, as a strategy to cope with increasing urban populations amidst negative impacts of climate change on the water resource. Most definitions of WDM assign the initiative for WDM to the service provider. One commonly used definition of WDM is '...adaptation and implementation of a strategy by a water institution to influence the water demand and usage in order to meet any of the following objectives: economic efficiency, social development, social equity, environmental protection, sustainability of water supply and services and political acceptability' (Jalil and Njiru, 2006, p.45). Under WDM, a service provider develops policies and invests in measures to achieve efficient water use both within the water distribution network (i.e. management of non-revenue water) and at the end-users' premises. However, water utilities would have no moral authority to urge end-users to conserve water in their properties, if they cannot reduce water losses within the distribution network.

Management of non-revenue water is of strategic importance to many water utilities in towns/cities of developing countries, where high levels of water losses in the water distribution networks have compromised effectiveness and efficiency of service delivery. For instance, performance assessment carried out under the auspices of the African Water Operators'

Partnerships (WOPs) found that the average level of non-revenue water (NRW) in 134 surveyed urban water service providers was 32 m³/km-day, 0.57 m³/connection-day and 36% of water delivered to the distribution network (WSP et al, 2009). In South Africa, NRW in 2005 was estimated to be 1.430 billion m³, which was 35.8% of total water input into the municipal distribution systems – hence, reduction of NRW has been singled out as the most viable immediate option in the short term to minimize water shortages in many areas (Mwiiga, Gumbo & Mkoka, 2010).

There are numerous benefits arising from successful implementation of WDM measures. Environmentally, WDM leads to reduced consumption of the dwindling water resource and minimizes the negative environmental impacts associated with water abstraction, treatment, distribution and use. Economically, satisfying new demand using water saved through WDM measures will have lower costs than exploiting new sources, and there will be savings through reduced operation and maintenance costs of the water supply system. From the social equity angle, water saved through WDM measures could be redistributed to urban residents who currently receive low service levels, hence moving closer to achievement of the Millennium Development Goal on water supply and sanitation. Technologically, WDM will provide incentives for developing water-saving equipment and devices.

In spite of the considerable potential benefits from effective management of NRW, relatively few utilities in the developed regions have put emphasis on implementing NRW programmes. One of the key constraints to the implementation of NRW is the lack of accurate information on the benefits of effective management of NRW – water engineers have sometimes not articulated well the financial benefits of reducing NRW, the language that managers understand best. Other key constraints are current mind sets and interests of politicians, water utility personnel, contractors and financiers biased for new infrastructure developments; inadequate policy and legislation framework; and inadequate human and financial resources, mainly as a result of under-priced water services (Jalil & Njiru, 2005). The remainder of this paper presents results of a case study that shows that in spite of many challenges, Ghana Water Company Ltd (GWCL), the water utility in Accra has implemented proactive measures to manage NRW in a systematic manner.

The study

One of the primary objectives of establishing private sector participation in Ghana's urban water sector in 2005 was to manage NRW more effectively, estimated to have been 52% in Accra at the start of the sector reforms (Nyarko, 2007). The objective of this study was to assess measures put in place to manage NRW more effectively in Accra. The study was conducted during the period June-August 2010. During a field trip to Accra in June 2010, the author became familiar with the research setting, identified relevant people to interview and collected useful official documents. The next field trip to Accra was in August 2010, during which interviews were conducted with key informants of GWCL, and observations carried out in the field.

The International Water Association (IWA) framework for good practices of water loss management was adapted for the assessment (Brothers, 2003). The following areas were assessed:

- overall network management;
- speed and quality of visible physical losses;
- active leakage management;
- pressure management;
- asset management;
- customer metering policy;
- reduction of water thefts;
- reduction of meter errors; and
- reduction of billing errors.

Nine interviews were conducted with key informants from the following departments/sections:

- GWCL headquarters;
- Regional offices, Accra West;
- Network management;
- Meter and instrumentation;
- Geographical Information Systems (GIS);
- Billing and Customer Care;
- Project management; and
- Asset management.

Background information

Accra is the capital city of Ghana, and is part of the Greater Accra Region, the smallest of the ten geographical regions of Ghana. The population in the Greater Accra Region was about 2.9 million in 2000, and is estimated to have increased to about 3.7m, assuming an urban growth rate of 4.4% (Ghana Statistical Services, 2005). Prior to the water sector restructuring in the 1990s, water and sanitation services in Accra were provided by Ghana Water and Sewerage Corporation (GWSC), which was also mandated to provide services to all rural and urban areas in Ghana. However, management of GWSC put more focus on urban services, and subsequently, the rural water department was converted into the semi-autonomous Community Water and Sanitation Department in 1994. Three major changes took place in 1998: the Community Water and Sanitation Department was transformed into the fully autonomous Community Water and Sanitation Agency (CWSA); the responsibility for urban sewerage and sanitation services was transferred to the District Assemblies; and GWSC was converted into a limited liability company, the Ghana Water Company Ltd (GWCL), with the responsibility for urban water supply only (Nyarko, 2007).

The second phase of restructuring aimed at separating service provision from regulation, and introduction of private sector participation in urban water services, so as to enhance public accountability, effectiveness and efficiency. The Public Utilities Regulatory Commission (PURC) and Water Resources Commission (WRC) were set up in 1998 to oversee delivery of water services and manage water resources respectively. After a long preparatory phase, a private water operator was appointed in 2005 on a five-year management contract (*ibid*). Aqua Vitens Rand Limited (AVRL), the operator, is a joint venture company between Vitens International Company (Holland) and Rand Water Services (South Africa). AVRL operates in 87 urban water supply systems scattered in all ten regions of Ghana and its main activities are abstraction of raw water, treatment to the required water quality standards, distribution to customers, billing and revenue collection.(AVRL, 2010). AVRL have decentralized service delivery to 12 operational regions. The region serving the capital city is Accra Tema Metropolitan Area (ATMA), composed of Accra West, Accra East and Tema service districts.

The total installed capacity in all the 87 urban water supply systems is 740,640m³/day, but the average daily production is 646,500m³/day. The estimated demand for potable water in these urban areas is 1,101,000m³/

day, meaning that even if there were no losses in the distribution network, the service coverage would be 59%. The NRW for all the water supply systems was estimated to be 47.6% in July 2010, down from 51.4% in 2009. However, NRW for ATMA was estimated at a higher figure of 58.5% (AVRL, 2010). By June 2010, GWCL had a total of about 430,000 customer connections, about half of these located in the ATMA, and growing at about 4% per annum. Domestic consumers make 85% of service connections, and contribute about 50% of revenue collection. Commercial and industrial customers, who constitute about 1% of the customer base, contribute about 34% of revenue collected.

Water supply for ATMA is provided by two main sources, the Kpong system on the River Volta and the Weija system on the River Densu, as shown in Figure 10.1. About 84% of residents in ATMA depend on piped water supplied by GWCL, and the remainder being serviced by systems managed by other providers such as the Community Water Supply Agency, and privately managed water schemes (e.g. WaterHealth Centres) (Ghana Statistical Services, 2008). In addition to providing services through connections to households and non-domestic properties, GWCL supplies water to small scale service providers i.e. public standpipe operators, tanker operators, sachet water producers and bottled water producers. Table 10.1 shows the customer base of GWCL in ATMA in 2007.

Table 10.1. Average number of AVRL customers in 2007									
Area	Tanker services	House-holds	Public Stand-pipes	Sachet water producers	Bottled water producers	Comm. sales	Industrial sales	Institutions (private)	Institutions (Gov't)
Accra East	1	57,342	74	0	1	11869	58	453	1057
Accra West	9	56,329	57	0	0	6515	65	653	336
Tema	4	40,647	494	218	3	7513	95	258	488
Total ATMA	14	154,318	625	218	4	25,897	218	1364	1881

Source: AVRL, 2008

163

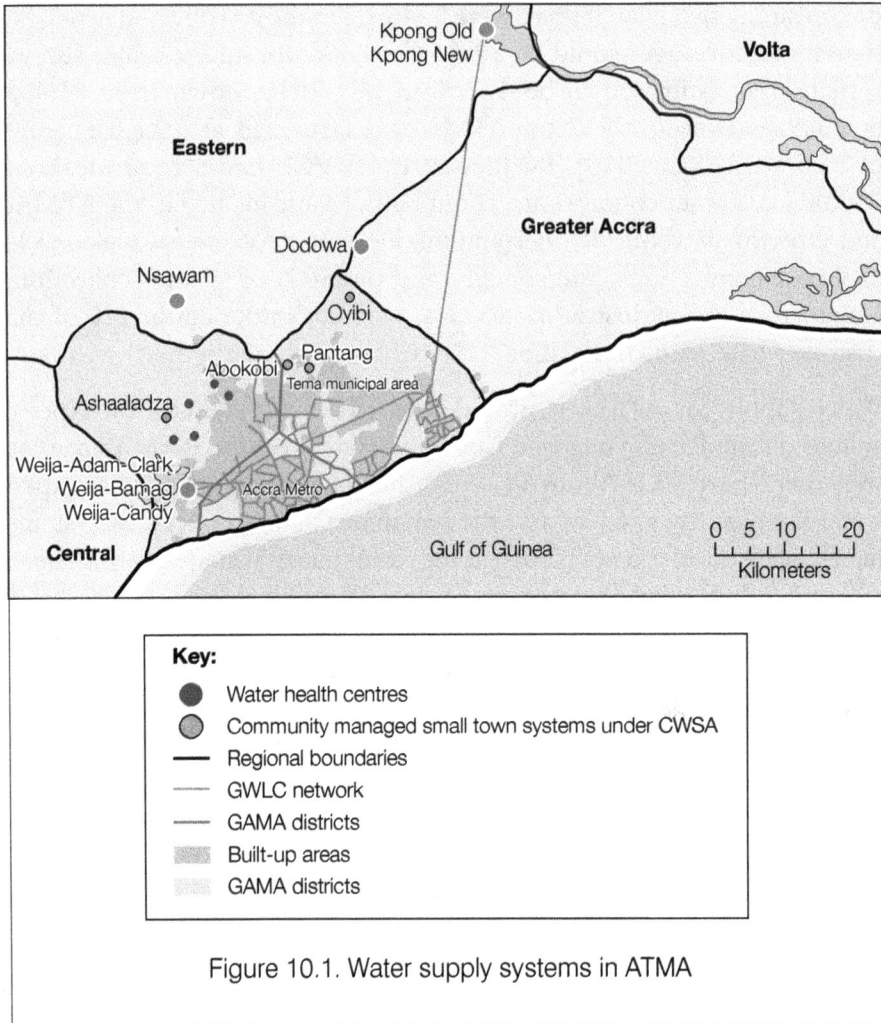

Figure 10.1. Water supply systems in ATMA

Key findings

Overall network management

The responsibility for network management falls under the Directorate of Water Operations, Monitoring and Asset Management, which is responsible for water production, water distribution monitoring, water operations, assets management and water quality monitoring. Network management in Accra falls under the Chief Operating Officer for ATMA. Theoretically, the ATMA distribution network is demarcated into three pressure zones, as follows:

- The Low Pressure Zone (LPZ) covering ground elevations between 0 – 30.5 m, above sea level, which services the largest part of the city. The LPZ is controlled by the water levels in the Weija works storage facilities to the west; in the Accra terminal reservoir (altitude 73 m) to the North; and in the Mile 4 reservoir (altitude 57 m) in the centre.

- The Medium Pressure Zone (MPZ), covering areas with ground elevation between 30.5 and 61m. The MPZ is normally controlled by the MPZ reservoir (altitude 97 m). However, at the time of the study, this reservoir was not in service, and the MPZ was being supplied directly from the HPZ booster station.

- The High Pressure Zone (HPZ) servicing areas with elevation of over 61m above sea level. This is controlled by the HPZ Reservoir, at an altitude of 137 m above sea level.

In practice, the supply zones are not well demarcated due to the intermittent water supply situation prevailing in the supply area. Nonetheless, GWCL is in the process of streamlining the sectorization, installing bulk meters and setting up DMAs, starting with Dansoman District. By the time of the study, six DMA had been set up. A Geographical Information System (GIS) unit was set up a couple of years back, and is in the process of digitizing the network. Currently, GWCL is in the process carrying out a network survey so that essential physical data could be uploaded into the GIS dataset.

Speed and quality of repair of bursts and leakages

GWCL has a service obligation to their customers to repair visible leaks that are reported within 48 hours. To improve the speed of repair and reduce physical water losses, GWCL started a 'visible leaks detection team' in 10 of the 14 districts in ATMA last year. Twenty plumbers working in the districts (usually artisans with national vocational training institute certificates in pipefitting) were trained on patrolling for leakages and bursts and using Global Positioning Systems (GPS) to create leakage maps. Based on demarcated smaller zones allocated to them, members of the team carry out inspections with cycles of about one month. The team members have been allocated official motorcycles, and are provided with tokens to recharge their mobile phones. The team member records the time when the leakage has been spotted and notes the location of the leakage, as picked up by the GPS. Members of the detection team carry out the repairs if they have the resources to handle the leakages. Alternatively, a report is immediately made to the larger repair team at district office. These data are transmitted to the GIS Unit, which stores them in a 'reported leakage' database and plots them onto a leakage map. The following information is captured:

- district;
- description of locality;
- material of the pipe, if known;
- date and time reported;
- name of officer reporting;
- the pipe size;
- classification of the pipeline (i.e. whether transmission, distribution or service line); and
- notes on peculiar aspects of the burst/leakage, if any.

To supplement the localized teams, there are two teams based at the GWCL headquarters which move around in official vehicles on the lookout for leakages. These teams also carry out repairs on leaks they can fix instantaneously, and report the unattended ones to the district offices. All the plumbers attend regular courses on workmanship for quality of the repairs and better customer relations. When repairs have been done, the local detection teams (who in many cases are also part of the repair team that fixes larger leakages) record the time when the repair has been accomplished, and when the network has been re-commissioned for supply. This information is then sent to the GIS Unit, which enters it into the 'repaired leakages' database, and updates the leakage maps. The following information is entered into the database:

- district;
- description of locality;
- material of pipe repaired;
- team leader of the group that carried out the repairs;
- size of the pipe;
- classification of the pipeline (i.e. whether transmission, distribution or service line);
- date and time of repair; and
- points of interest noted during the repair event, if any.

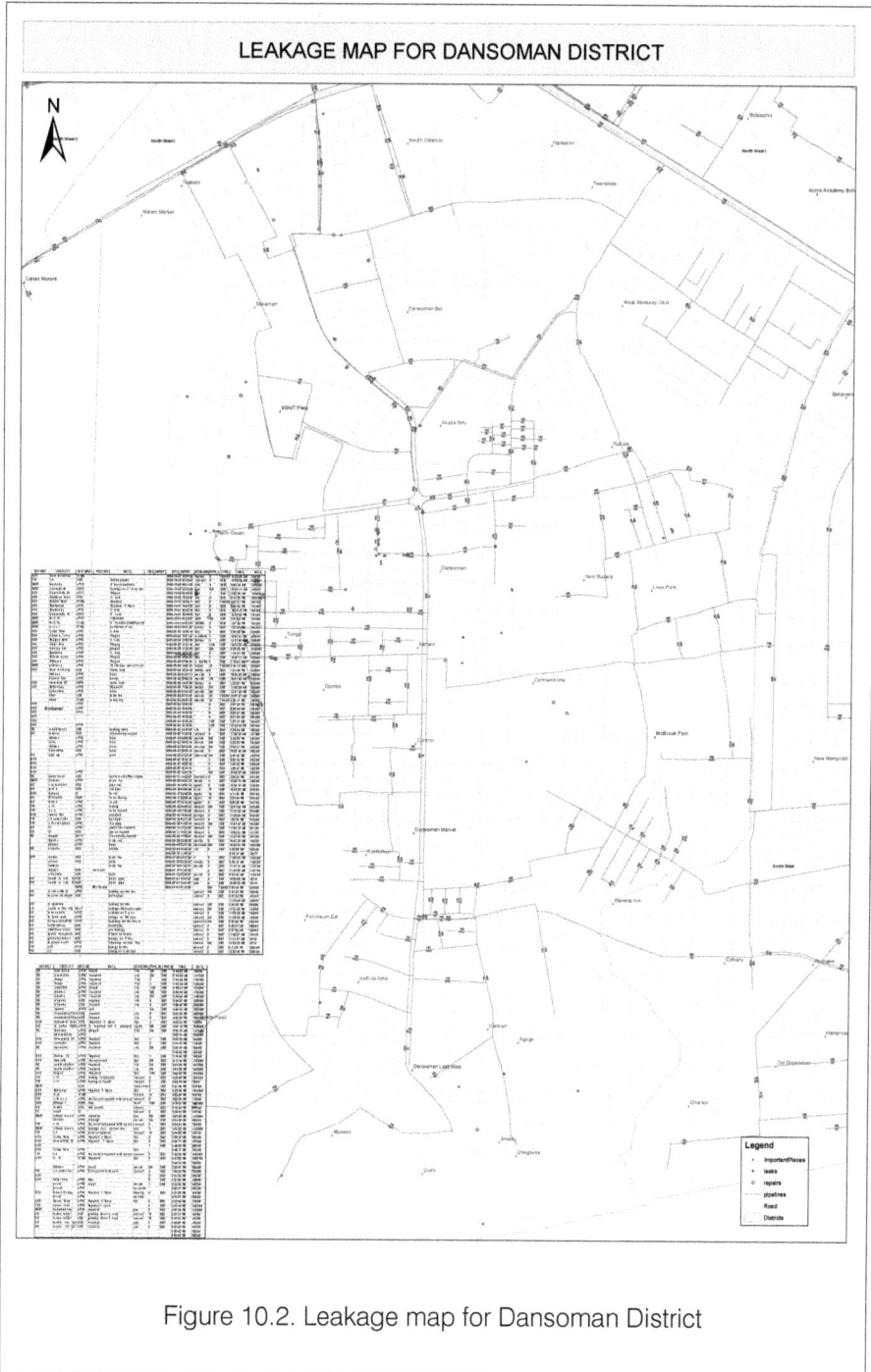

Figure 10.2. Leakage map for Dansoman District

Figure 10.2 shows an example of a leakage map plotted for Dansoman District, with sections of the database superimposed on it. The red dots represent reported leaks and the green dots represent repaired leaks. This programme was due to be reviewed in September 2010, a year after it had been operational, with a view of scaling it up.

Setting up of district meter areas

GWCL started setting up District Meter Areas (DMAs) in September 2009 and, by the time of the study, six DMAs had been commissioned in Dansoman District of ATMA region, where the distribution network has already been digitized. Initially, DMAs are being set up with no more than 1000 property accounts, to enable technicians to start with smaller areas which will be easier to handle, as they gain experience. Prior to pressure testing, DMA plots are produced showing the position of all meters, inlet and boundary valves, flushing and pressure tapping points. Using Primayer data loggers, zero pressure tests were carried out to establish the integrity of the DMAs. A minimum of seven days' pressure and flow data for those DMAs that passed the zero pressure tests were analysed for consistency before they were commissioned as fully operational DMAs. The first generation of DMAs was commissioned in April 2010.

Manuals were prepared for all commissioned DMAs. A DMA manual identifies the location of the DMA in terms of water supply zone and water operational area. It also describes the process and date of commissioning. Pressure and flow graphs generated prior to commissioning are documented, as well as a description of any problems encountered. Other information included, and continuously updated is:

- data sets of the customers in the DMA, such as type of customer and size of service connection;
- details of physical characteristics of the DMA such as lengths, diameters and material of the pipeline;
- all meter information, such as type, serial number, pulse unit required for logging, date of installation etc;
- status of data logging, i.e. whether
- available logging (DMA in operation and data logger currently deployed), or
- available no logging (DMA in operation but no data logger deployed), or

- unavailable (there is a problem with the meter; hence data on water usage may NOT be obtained); and
- flow and pressure readings

Data from DMAs whose status is 'available logging' is downloaded periodically and manuals updated with graphs of flows and pressures, hence providing data for analysis to determine the leakage levels over a period of time. By the time of the study, GWCL was updating data of the commissioned DMAs. The next stage will be to analyse leakage patterns and start active leakage detection.

Reduction of meter under-registration errors

In many water utilities of the developing regions, meter under-registration usually contributes a significant portion of apparent losses, sometimes referred to as commercial losses or administration losses. Meter under-registration takes place when a customer's meter fails to accurately measure flows, especially the lower flows. Meter under-registration tends to increase with time and as the meter gets older. There are several types of meters in service, each with their own characteristics, such as volumetric, single-jet, multi-jet, turbine, woltmann, smart meters etc. To reduce these errors, the service provider needs to have a meter maintenance workshop that has appropriate meter testing equipment and well trained staff.

Although the meter workshop has been in place since the establishment of Ghana Water and Sewerage Corporation, it was not fully functional, mainly because tools and equipment were not replaced, and staff were not continuously trained and/or adequately incentivized. With the advent of AVRL as the operator, the meter workshop was rehabilitated, and new testing instruments installed. An intensive training programme was conducted in early 2008, targeting nine meter workshop staff in Accra and Kumasi. The first part of the training programme dealt with basic concepts such as working principles and different types of water meters; and dismantling, cleaning, overhauling and mounting of meters. The second part covered verification and calibration of meters; working principles of test benches; calibration tanks; compilation of deviation and error curves.

Requisitions for meter servicing are received from the Customer Care Office. The meter workshop staff carry out the following roles:

- repairing of faulty meters;
- testing and calibrating old and new meters;
- carrying out field tests on bulk and service meters; and

- keeping an accurate record of meters installed and/or removed for repairs.

GWCL has streamlined the procurement process to ensure that purchase of meters is standardized. Currently, GWCL is mainly using horizontal Woltmann meters and multi-jet OPTIMA meters. The meter workshop has strict procedures for handling of received meters, to maintain safety and integrity of the meter parts. The data recorded in the meter workshop database include Account number, account name, meter serial number, seal number, brand and size, final reading (for meter removed), initial reading (for meter installed), name of meter serviceman, spare parts used, labour input, and meter status (whether repaired or scrapped). Given a staff strength of six, the meter workshop in Accra could clean and assemble up to 100 metres per day, but only 54 meters can be tested in a working day, due to the fixed timings of some bench-testing procedures. Figure 10.3 shows some of the tasks undertaken in the meter workshop.

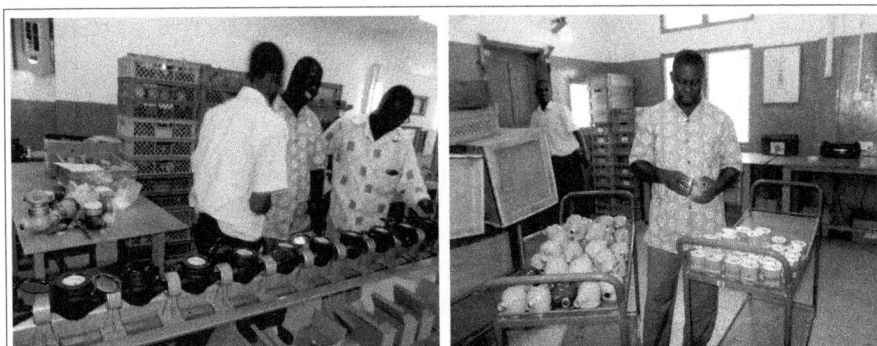

Figure 10.3. Meter workshop staff assembling clean meters and the test bench, August 2010

Reduction of other apparent (commercial) losses

Apart from meter under-registration, other components of apparent losses or commercial losses are metre reading errors, water theft and water accounting errors. Meter reading errors may be unintended, or through collusion of meter readers and customers; water thefts usually consist of bypasses to the water meters, illegal connections or wilful damage to the water meter. Water accounting errors are billing anomalies that may occur intentionally, say through collusion of billing staff and customers. They may also be as a result of human errors (manual or computer input errors) or anomalies such as non-volumetric estimates that do not reflect actual consumption values.

The management of GWCL recognized the fact that other than contacts through meter readers, the utility did not know their customers well enough, which is not only detrimental to customer relations, but also fuels illegal connections. Consequently, a research section was set up in the Customer Care Department, with the objective of mapping customers using GPS equipment and continuously upgrading the electronic customer database. The task forces operating under the Customer Research Section have identified cases of water thefts, falling into the category of those who are registered as GWCL customers who have been disconnected for non-payment, but reconnected illegally. Such customers are asked to pay regularization charges, failure of which leads the utility to consider taking litigation measures.

Another category of water thefts is consumers who are connected illegally to the water distribution network, but they have never applied to the utility for a connection at all. In such cases, the utility usually grants an amnesty for them to pay for only a connection fee within a period of two weeks. If they do not respond positively within the specified period, they are expected to pay for the water estimated to have been consumed in the past, a connection fee, and a penalty fee, of say about 200 Ghana Cedes. If they do not comply, GWCL considers litigation measures against the illegal consumers. However, owing to the slow judicial process, GWCL prefers to exhaust all other methods before resorting to litigation measures.

The data collected by the Customer Research Section are also used to assess the consistency of meter readings. Once the mapping has been accomplished, meter readings are taken and compared with data recently recorded in the meter dockets for consistency. Recent assessment exercises have found anomalies with between 50-60% of the sampled meter readings. As a follow up, new demand notices with the correct information are sent to customers, and the responsible meter readers are cautioned. Where the anomalies are significant, the meter reader's operational areas are systematically checked for consistency of meter readings.

Results of the customer mapping exercise show that there is a large margin of error in bills that are based on estimated consumption, highlighting the need to aim for universal metering. Hence, GWCL has intensified the metering exercise. At the time of the study, GWCL was in an advanced stage of awarding a contract for fitting 34,000 meters in ATMA and other operational regions. As of June 2010, Accra East and Accra West had accomplished 60% metering coverage. The coverage in Tema sub-region was better, at an estimated 95%, mainly because it is easier to deal with, given the fact that it is predominantly industrial. At the time of the study, GWCL was reconsidering the option of installing prepaid meters in low income settlements, which were tried in the 1990s, but were unsuccessful, mainly because 'software' aspects of the user communities were not properly managed.

There are other benefits associated with the customer mapping exercise. By carrying out a property-to-property assessment, instances of double counting have been discovered, whereby some properties which are serviced by the CWSA were still appearing in the GWCL database. Subsequently, the 'ghost' customers have been removed. For instance, the total number of GWCL customers was estimated to be 460,160 as of May 2006. As a result of the customer mapping exercise, some customer accounts were weeded out, and the number fell to about 430,000 by June 2010. Another spin-off benefit is that whenever leakages are encountered, information is instantly passed on to the District Area office for appropriate action.

As a way of minimizing water thefts, GWCL has also intensified public education. Stakeholder forums are held regularly to educate customers on the importance of cost recovery for providing good service levels. Organized groups such as local district assemblies, community-based organizations and church groups are targeted. Public education for the youth (especially from high schools) has been intensified, and they are showcased the water treatment processes, so that they may appreciate cost implications, change their mindsets, and act as change agents in the homes. Promotion fliers are occasionally attached to the bills, and GWCL are in partnership with various electronic/print media houses to communicate the message about the importance of cost recovery.

To reduce water accounting errors, GWCL has developed in-house software to check the consistency of data from various databases. Queries are generated from time to time if anomalies are spotted. Furthermore, Utility/2000, the software used for customer management systems is continuously upgraded, and there are plans to replace it with new software that has a bigger capacity, higher efficiency, and with more functionality. To reduce collusion between staff and customers, billing units that previously used to sit in the district offices have been centralized to regional offices. To reduce human errors, staff training has been intensified, thanks to the establishment of an IT training centre in early 2010. New staff with more modern skills are being recruited to boost the capacity of existing billing staff. Furthermore, a new organization structure that became effective in mid 2010 has a provision for closer supervision of meter reading and billing functions. Up to two staff in each district will be responsible for checking meter readings and carrying out evaluation of the billing process.

Asset management

An Asset Management Manager (AMM) was appointed in early 2010, whose major task is to develop and maintain asset planning and asset tracking systems that ensure effective maintenance of the company assets. At the time of the study, the AMM had not yet taken full responsibility. Functions for management of assets were still spread over various GWCL departments. An immediate task of the AMM is to ensure centralization of most aspects of asset management, and carry out an asset evaluation, to update the asset database created in 1996 when a comprehensive evaluation was last done.

Way forward

On the whole, GWCL is doing a good job to reduce NRW. It is impressive that there are multi-pronged interventions to reduce both commercial losses and physical losses, as this is the most effective way of managing NRW. However, minimal work is being done in the area of pressure management, mainly because the demarcation of the three pressure zones is not designed to function under intermittent water supply situations. It would be useful to redesign the water supply system to develop pressure zones that optimize the available level of supply with people driven levels of service objectives (Totsuka, Trifunovic & Vairavamoorthy, 2004). It is planned to carry out network evaluation in a more systematic manner. There is a need to also carry out regular water balances so that categories of water losses can be more accurately pinpointed. This requires regular calibration of bulk meters.

Most of the tasks for reduction of NRW are part of ongoing time-bound externally-funded projects. There is a need to mainstream these activities into the normal operation and maintenance tasks, so that they could outgrow the lifetime of the projects. Some staff have been trained under various project components to carry out water loss management. Training should be mainstreamed in the utility corporate services, so that it is continuous and beneficial to all relevant staff. Furthermore, there is a need to have more active linkages between the operation and maintenance departments managed by AVRL and the newly created Asset Management Department at GWCL headquarters.

As already stated, there are few water utilities in the developing regions which have invested enough resources to reduce NRW. GWCL management have shown a determination to tackle water losses in a multi-pronged approach, in spite of the inadequate level of resources in the company. NRW in Accra is in excess of 50%, which could create situations of complacency and resignation. This case study shows that no matter how insurmountable the task looks, management can rally resources to set up systems to manage NRW. It is anticipated that when the evaluation is carried out, it will show a significant improvement in the operational areas where the interventions are targeted. This is a case study that emphasizes the point that 'every little helps'.

References

Aqua Vitens Rand Limited (AVRL) (2008), *AVRL database data of 2007 production and sales data*, Accra, Ghana.

Aqua Vitens Rand Limited (AVRL) (2010) *Business Plan 2010*, Accra, Ghana.

Brothers, K. (2003) A practical approach to water loss management, *Water21, Magazine of the IWA*, June 2003, pp. 54-55.

Ghana Statistical Services (2005) *Analysis of district data and implications for planning Greater Accra Region*, Accra, Ghana.

Ghana Statistical Services (2008) *Report of the fifth round of the Ghana Living Standards Survey*.

Jalil, M.A. and Njiru, C. (2005) *Overcoming constraints to implementation of Water Demand Management in Urban Water Supplies*, unpublished paper, WEDC, Loughborough University, UK.

Jalil, M.A. and Njiru, C. (2006) Water Demand Management in Urban Water Supplies – Present and Future Challenges, in: Rahman, M.M., Bin Alam, M.J., Ali, M.A. and Smout, I. (eds), *Environmental Sustainability Concerns*, pp.43-57, Environmental Engineering Division (EED), Centre for Environmental and Resource Management (CERM), and International Training Network (ITN) Centre, Bangladesh University of Engineering and Technology, Dhaka, Bangladesh.

Mwiinga, G., Gumbo, T. and Mkoka, I. (2010) Water conservation and water demand management in practice – South Africa case studies,in: *The Water Institute of Southern Africa (WISA) 2010 Biennial Conference and Exhibition*, Durban, South Africa.

Nyarko, K.B. (2007) *Drinking water sector in Ghana: drivers for performance*, PhD thesis, UNESCO-IHE, Taylor & Francis, Holland.

Totsuka, N., Trifunovic, N. & Vairavamoorthy, K. (2004) Intermittent urban water supply under water starving situations, in: *Proceedings of the 30th WEDC International Conference, Vientiane, Lao PDR, October 2004*. WEDC, Loughborough University, UK.

WSP; UN-HABITAT; IWA-East and Southern Africa Region (ESAR) and African Water Association (AfWA) (2009) *Water Operators Partnerships: Africa Utility Performance Assessment*, Water and Sanitation Program – Africa, Nairobi, Kenya available at http://www.unhabitat.org/downloads/docs/WOP_Report.pdf [accessed 19 January 2011]

www.ingramcontent.com/pod-product-compliance
Lightning Source LLC
Chambersburg PA
CBHW080249030426
42334CB00023BA/2751